The Rise and Fall of the Taliban

Other books in the At Issue in History series:

The Rise and Fall of the Taliban

Kelly Barth, *Book Editor*

Bruce Glassman, *Vice President*
Bonnie Szumski, *Publisher*
Helen Cothran, *Managing Editor*
Scott Barbour, *Series Editor*

 **AT ISSUE IN HISTORY**

GREENHAVEN PRESS
An imprint of Thomson Gale, a part of The Thomson Corporation

Detroit • New York • San Francisco • San Diego • New Haven, Conn.
Waterville, Maine • London • Munich

LIBRARY OF CONGRESS CATALOGING-IN-PUBLICATION DATA

The rise and fall of the Taliban / Kelly Barth, book editor.
    p. cm. — (At issue in history)
  Includes bibliographical references and index.
  ISBN 0-7377-1987-7 (lib. : alk. paper)
    1. Taliban. 2. Afghanistan—History—1989–2001. I. Barth, Kelly. II. Series.
  DS371.3.R58 2005
  958.104'6—dc22   2003067515

Printed in the United States of America

Contents

relative, and were denied basic rights to employment, health care, and education.

Chapter 3: The U.S. War and the Fall of the Taliban

tion and that of the Afghani civilians who survive
the attacks.

Foreword

Historian Robert Weiss defines history simply as "a record and interpretation of past events." Both elements—record and interpretation—are necessary, Weiss argues.

> Names, dates, places, and events are the essence of history. But historical writing is not a compendium of facts. It consists of facts placed in a sequence to tell a connected story. A work of history is not merely a story, however. It also must analyze what happened and *why*—that is, it must interpret the past for the reader.

For example, the events of December 7, 1941, that led President Franklin D. Roosevelt to call it "a date which will live in infamy" are fairly well known and straightforward. A force of Japanese planes and submarines launched a torpedo and bombing attack on American military targets in Pearl Harbor, Hawaii. The surprise assault sank five battleships, disabled or sank fourteen additional ships, and left almost twenty-four hundred American soldiers and sailors dead. On the following day, the United States formally entered World War II when Congress declared war on Japan.

These facts and consequences were almost immediately communicated to the American people who heard reports about Pearl Harbor and President Roosevelt's response on the radio. All realized that this was an important and pivotal event in American and world history. Yet the news from Pearl Harbor raised many unanswered questions. Why did Japan decide to launch such an offensive? Why were the attackers so successful in catching America by surprise? What did the attack reveal about the two nations, their people, and their leadership? What were its causes, and what were its effects? Political leaders, academic historians, and students look to learn the basic facts of historical events and to read the intepretations of these events by many different sources, both primary and secondary, in order to develop a more complete picture of the event in a historical context.

In the case of Pearl Harbor, several important questions surrounding the event remain in dispute, most notably the role of President Roosevelt. Some historians have blamed his policies for deliberately provoking Japan to attack in order to propel America into World War II; a few have gone so far as to accuse him of knowing of the impending attack but not informing others. Other historians, examining the same event, have exonerated the president of such charges, arguing that the historical evidence does not support such a theory.

The Greenhaven At Issue in History series recognizes that many important historical events have been interpreted differently and in some cases remain shrouded in controversy. Each volume features a collection of articles that focus on a topic that has sparked controversy among eyewitnesses, contemporary observers, and historians. An introductory essay sets the stage for each topic by presenting background and context. Several chapters then examine different facets of the subject at hand with readings chosen for their diversity of opinion. Each selection is preceded by a summary of the author's main points and conclusions. A bibliography is included for those students interested in pursuing further research. An annotated table of contents and thorough index help readers to quickly locate material of interest. Taken together, the contents of each of the volumes in the Greenhaven At Issue in History series will help students become more discriminating and thoughtful readers of history.

Introduction

In less than a decade during the 1990s, the Taliban, a previously unknown Islamic fundamentalist political group, rose to prominence and power and conquered most of Afghanistan. During its rise to power, the organization attracted a great deal of international attention due to its imposition of a strict version of Islamic law and its purported human rights abuses. After September 11, 2001, the world's focus on the Taliban quickly intensified because the group was indirectly implicated in the terrorist attacks on New York; Washington, D.C.; and Pennsylvania. Though to many the Taliban may have seemed a fringe group of extremists who came out of nowhere to suddenly appear on the international stage, Afghanistan's long history of civil, religious, and political unrest had laid the groundwork for just such an organization to thrive.

Sources of Instability

For a combination of reasons, Afghanistan has long been vulnerable to manipulation and occupation by foreign powers and to takeover by fundamentalist groups such as the Taliban. One reason is the country's unique geography. Afghanistan is a land of mountainous desert interspersed with fertile river valleys and oases. Throughout the country's history, its people have been separated into distinct tribal groups by these physical boundaries of mountain ranges and large areas of inhospitable desert terrain. As a result, each distinct group or tribe has developed its own unique dialect, traditions, and beliefs. This has contributed to the Afghan people's difficulty seeing themselves as one nation and has kept them from defending themselves as such.

Another reason the country has been vulnerable to invasion by foreign powers is while it lacks significant natural resources of its own, it lies in the middle of a resource-rich region. Many foreign peoples have wanted to safely pass through Afghanistan to conduct trade. Consequently, those who controlled Afghanistan controlled not only the resources it possessed but also the flow of goods across it. This high-traffic trade route between India, Russia, western Asia, and ultimately Europe was called the Silk Route.

It is no surprise then, with its geography and location in the path of such a heavily traveled area, that Afghanistan has a long history of being destabilized by foreign invaders. One of the earliest recorded invasions took place in 330 B.C. when Alexander the Great, the Greek conquerer, invaded and subdued the country. This invasion opened up the area for Arab Muslim armies, who invaded Afghanistan from present-day Iran. By 654 these Muslims had begun converting most of the Afghan people to Islam. As the Muslims left the country, the Afghan people once again developed power structures of their own. Local Afghan control was quickly overturned once again in 1219 by Ghengis Khan, whose army moved into the region from Mongolia. This frequent pattern of invasions by foreign powers and takeovers by the dominant tribal groups in Afghanistan continued until the middle of the eighteenth century.

None of these foreign invaders was ever entirely successful at uniting the country under one kingdom or government. The presence of many beliefs and acquired cultural practices among the distinct tribes and subtribes in Afghanistan made it difficult for conquerors who tried to do so. As journalist Ahmed Rashid says in his book *Taliban: Militant Islam, Oil, and Fundamentalism in Central Asia*, "This series of invasions resulted in a complex ethnic, cultural and religious mix that was to make Afghan nation-building extremely difficult."[1] Due to the country's blend of ethnic, tribal, and subtribal identities, the people belong to any one of eight generally recognized groups: the Pashtuns, Tajiks, Hazara, Uzbeks, Baluchis, Turkmen, Aimaqs, and Kirghiz.

In 1747 one of these tribal groups was able to rise to power, for the first time in the history of the region, to shape Afghanistan into a nation in its own right. The Pashtun tribe to the south, the largest ethnic group in the country, asserted its dominance. The Pashtun leader Ahmad Shah Durrani managed to hold military control over the rest of the country. This unification did not last long, however. Half a century after Durrani's death, fighting over the legitimacy of his government ensued, and the country's tribal areas became embroiled in civil war. This conflict left the country vulnerable to foreign invasion once again. This time the players were two of the world's imperialist powers, Great Britain and Russia.

The Great Game

Great Britain and Russia both saw Afghanistan as strategic to their political interests. Since about 1600, Britain had had great economic and political interest in India. By the middle of the nineteenth century, Britain had taken over the entire Indian subcontinent and its government. The British knew that protecting their territory in India would involve keeping a close eye on their competitor, Russia. Similarly, Russia feared British expansion into Central Asia, including the crucial buffer country of Afghanistan. The bitter conflict between the two world powers became known as the Great Game.

Weakened by its own civil war and left once again without a central government, Afghanistan was taken advantage of by both countries, but especially by Britain. Britain invaded the country in 1838 and again in 1849 under the guise of adding stability to the war-torn country, but primarily to keep Russia from invading and threatening its interests in India. Known as the Anglo-Afghan Wars, the conflicts left Afghanistan under British rule from the middle of the nineteenth century until the early part of the twentieth century.

During the British occupation Afghanistan's borders changed in ways that would cause it further conflict in the future. In 1893 the British established a firm boundary between India and Afghanistan called the Durand Line, named after the British Indian foreign secretary, Sir Mortimer Durand, under whose watch the boundary was established. This border did not take into account the ethnic makeup of the region and consequently has exacerbated ethnic tensions in the area. In the early twentieth century, Britain was reeling from costly involvement in World War I. It no longer had the resources to defend as much colonial territory. Afghanistan was granted independence from Britain in 1919.

Afghanistan Turns to the Soviets

Once again Afghanistan was on its own to try to manage major conflicts but without the necessary national unity. Following World War II Britain was unable to suppress uprisings in India and in 1947 granted India complete independence. The Muslim population of the Northwest Frontier Province then chose to break away from India and form the country of Pakistan. The British-established Durand Line, which formed Afghanistan's southern border, also cut through the center of the ancestral territory of the nomadic and fiercely independent Pashtun tribe. Border disputes arose between the Pashtuns and the new country of Pakistan over who had rightful claim to the territory. By 1950 the conflict had escalated to such a level that trade relations ended between the two countries. This development cut Afghanistan off from much needed imports of petroleum and dealt a heavy blow to its economy.

The conflict with Pakistan made way for a mutually beneficial relationship to blossom between Afghanistan and the Soviet Union. In the 1940s the two countries became trading partners. In the 1950s and 60s, in exchange for oil and gas exploration rights in northern Afghanistan, the Soviet Union built military airfields in Afghanistan and provided the country with arms and ammunition to protect its borders. This assistance, however, did little to alleviate the border conflicts between the Pashtuns and Pakistanis. In 1961 Pakistan severed all diplomatic ties with Afghanistan and refused to allow the nomadic Pashtuns to cross into their historic tribal area across the Pakistani border.

By the late 1960s the relationship between the Soviet Union and Afghanistan had already begun to sour. Tribal conflicts in Afghanistan continued to prevent the country's unification. In 1967 the leading political organization, the People's Democratic Party of Afghanistan (PDPA), was split due to conflicts between its two leaders, Nur Mohammad Taraki and Babrak Karmal. Taraki, leader of the largely rural Khalq faction, was Pashtun. Karmal, leader of the Parcham faction, drew followers who were much more cosmopolitan and multiethnic.

By 1973 internal political turmoil and external pressure from the Soviet Union and Pakistan had further destabilized Afghanistan. In a military coup, the former prime minister of Afghanistan, Sardar Mohammad Daud Khan, took over the country from King Zahir Shah. Then in 1978 the PDPA launched a military coup and took over the country, putting Taraki in power as president. The Parcham faction questioned Taraki's leadership. In 1979 Hafizullah Amin, a member of the Khalq faction, assassinated Taraki and installed himself as leader. He resisted Soviet offers of help in stabilizing the country.

The Soviet Occupation

Unable to rely on Afghanistan's own Communist organization, the PDPA, to manage its own internal conflicts, the Soviet Union became another in a series of foreign governments to try to subdue the country. Believing that the region was crucial to its economic and political interests, the Soviet Union invaded Afghanistan in December 1979. The Soviets had another compelling motivation: They wanted to prevent the funding and spread of anti-Communist, Islamic opposition groups that were gaining strength throughout the country.

During the decade of their occupation of Afghanistan, Soviet forces battled these Islamic opposition groups, called the mujahideen, whose members believed it a holy duty to oust the infidel Soviets from their country. Most of these Islamic fundamentalists were based in the neighboring Islamic countries of Iran and Pakistan, where they established refugee camps. There they were educated, armed, and prepared to make warring excursions into Afghanistan.

Pakistan took the stage as yet another foreign power interested in controlling Afghanistan, and it did so by supporting the mujahideen movement. The country's leaders wanted to create an Islamic bloc from Pakistan to Central Asia that would protect them against India. They also had interest in joining forces with anyone who wanted to help them oust the Soviets entrenched along their border. Pakistan agreed to recognize and financially support seven larger groups of mujahideen resistance parties in Afghanistan, four of which were Islamic and three of which were made up of traditional tribal leaders in Afghanistan. Each group generally held ideological sway over a particular region.

Countries around the world condemned the Soviet invasion. Not surprisingly, this group included the United States, the Soviet Union's longtime rival. Rather than engage in direct conflict with the Soviets, which could have resulted in a nuclear war, the United States instead began to fund the mujahideen to fight against them. As part of its covert mission in Afghanistan, President Ronald Reagan's administration (1981–1989) supplied missiles to the mujahideen to shoot down Soviet aircraft.

The decade of Soviet occupation took a heavy toll on the people of Afghanistan. So many Afghans fled to border countries such as Iran, Pakistan, and India to escape the battles between the Soviets and resistance forces that the country remained in a constant state of economic and cultural upheaval. Also, frequent long droughts and famines during this decade forced the primarily rural Hazara people of central and northeastern Afghanistan into densely packed urban areas, where they knew they could receive Soviet government subsidies. This migration put people with vastly different tribal customs and religious beliefs in close proximity and into direct conflict with each other.

The Soviets were no more successful than earlier foreign powers had been at uniting Afghanistan. Trying to do so was more costly than politically beneficial. Because of its occupation of Afghanistan, the Soviet Union was cut off diplomatically from many other countries in the world. Faced with this economic and political isolation and the rising military cost it would have to expend to continue to try to subdue Afghanistan, the Soviet Union began to contemplate ending the occupation. In 1987 Soviet president Mikhail Gorbachev entered talks with UN peace negotiators and representatives from Pakistan, the United States, and the Soviet-sponsored Afghan government. The mujahideen, however, were excluded from the talks. The Soviets remained in the country until 1989, when they finally admitted they had been defeated in their attempts to secure the country under a Communist government.

Another Governmental Void

Unfortunately for the Afghan people, the Soviets left without providing adequate support to the transitional government and left their country completely destabilized. Against both Pakistani and U.S. wishes that the mujahideen be made integral to the new government, the Soviets put liberal leader Mohammad Najibullah in the presidency. Though Najibullah's government maintained control in major cities such as Kabul, Mazar-e Sharif, Kandahar, Herat, and Jalalabad, the mujahideen controlled the countryside and frequently attacked these urban enclaves.

Not only did the seven mujahideen groups fight the Najibullah government, they quickly lost solidarity with each other and abandoned any attempts to share power.

Fighting between mujahideen factions made rural areas dangerous. Villager turned against villager. Traditional methods of tribal peacekeeping became ineffective. Remaining refugees who had been staying in Pakistan and Iran flooded back into the country, increasing the mujahideen's fears that they would be unable to maintain control over their regions. Civil war broke out as the capital city of Kabul became an open battleground between mujahideen groups vying for control over the country.

Afghanistan was in a shambles. The infrastructure was already damaged from fighting the Soviets. Ravaged by nearly a decade of war, the economy had all but collapsed. Many were forced to become refugees in search of limited shelter and resources. Afghanistan could not have been more prepared for the promises of the Taliban, a coalition of disillusioned young men frustrated with years of strife and with the ineffectuality of the mujahideen.

The Taliban had been trained by the mujahideen in the refugee camps. There its members memorized and recited the Koran, the Muslim scriptures, and learned not only how to fight but what to fight: the corruption caused by Western ideas and customs. These young men, like most people under chronic civil distress, were vulnerable to fundamentalist ideas; a return to absolutes seemed the best defense against moral and political problems.

The Taliban Fills the Void

Though it seems to have risen out of nowhere, the Taliban actually had many ideological predecessors. For example, clear parallels can be drawn between the Taliban and the Wahhabi movement in Saudi Arabia. Concerned about what he considered a weakening of Islam, Wahhabism's founder Muhammad ibn 'Abd al-Wahhab (1703–1792) reigned Saudi Arabia with an iron hand, prohibiting music and dancing, making prayer and worship mandatory, and endorsing jihad as a way to eradicate corruption. Created in 1928, the Muslim Brotherhood similarly tried to counter the influence of Marxism among Muslims in Egypt. Members of the brotherhood believed religion should affect all aspects of life. Many members also believed that Muslims could, under the banner of Islam, attack people or their property justifiably if they were not believers or had turned from sharia, or Islamic law.

In 1994 the Taliban emerged in Kandahar as a small,

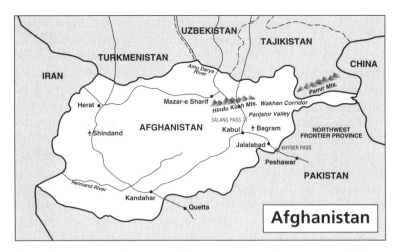

loosely organized group of young men who espoused fundamentalist Islam and who were determined to put an end to the instability brought about by fighting among the mujahideen. Their early military successes and demonstrated ability to stabilize Afghanistan where the mujahideen had failed soon garnered them backing from Pakistan, the Saudis, and even the United States—all countries with interests in the region.

Many rural Afghans had hoped that an Islamic government would be established to restore long-absent stability. Consequently, as frightening as they may have seemed to the outside world, the Taliban was initially well received in areas it conquered. As the group moved from region to region, many young men who had lived as refugees joined its ranks because, as human rights advocate Michael Renner says, "For many, joining up with the Taliban meant gaining a degree of importance and self-respect for the first time in their lives."[2]

Just as many Afghans had once hoped, the Taliban governed the country by sharia, which they interpreted very strictly. Sharia allowed the Taliban's religious police to deliver harsh punishments such as stoning of adulterers and amputations for theft. To enforce *hejab*, or the seclusion that the Taliban believed sharia required of Muslim women, the religious police required all women to wear the burka, a full-length, dark-colored garment that covers the whole body, any time they left their home. Women could not work, and girls could no longer attend school. Men were required to grow beards, wear expensive turbans, and attend daily prayer. Music, dancing, and nonreligious art were forbidden.

By winter 1995 the Taliban had taken over half of Afghanistan. In 1996 it invaded the capital of Kabul, dragged President Najibullah and his brother from a protected UN compound, and hanged them. The Taliban's harsh policies did provide some stability, but they were also beginning to take a toll on the population. Though the more traditional people in rural areas suffered under the Taliban's edicts, they understood and complied with them. People in cities, however, who had long enjoyed a more Western lifestyle, were hardly prepared for the Taliban's new rules. Conversely, disgusted by what they perceived as the ultimate corruption, the Taliban's religious police delivered much harsher punishments in urban areas.

Though extremely successful at using military force both to conquer and disarm civilian populations and enforce military law and order, the Taliban had the same difficulty organizing a government that all others had had before them. The religious police were often more violent than more moderate leaders would condone, and disagreements about how to govern broke out. The chain of command was always unclear. Over time, this disorganization began to increase people's fear of their new rulers.

As the Taliban continued to move north, bent on conquering the entire country, it created a humanitarian crisis it could no longer manage. Before invading an area, it would evacuate the civilian population and send the people to an already crowded and impoverished Kabul so it could fight resistance forces without civilian casualties. Finally, by 2000 the Taliban was losing control over the people it had conquered. It had to forcibly recruit young men to replace its ranks, and many young men fled the country to escape conscription.

Also, the support the Taliban had once enjoyed from foreign powers with interests in the region was waning. Early in the Taliban's history, Pakistan had seen many advantages to gaining the group's favor. Not only did Pakistan like the idea of an Islamic neighbor, the stability the Taliban provided allowed Pakistan to safely send goods along important trade routes. Pakistan, the United Arab Emirates, and Saudi Arabia also negotiated with the Taliban in the hopes of securing the right to build an oil pipeline from

Turkmenistan through Afghanistan and into Pakistan and India, squeezing out their competitor Iran. In the early years of the Taliban's reign, Pakistan acknowledged the group as the government of Afghanistan.

Though less willing to give official sanction to the Taliban because of reported human rights abuses, the United States had hopes of establishing friendly relations with the Taliban early in its rule as well. In fact, some accounts claim that the United States may have even cooperated with Pakistan and Saudi Arabia to ensure the Taliban took over the entire country of Afghanistan. The United States saw the Taliban as a stabilizing force that it could negotiate with to ensure that an oil and gas pipeline could be built by an American oil company, which would keep the nations of Iran and Russia from controlling the flow of oil. However, as U.S. officials became increasingly fearful of Osama bin Laden, a wealthy Islamic radical and leader of a terrorist organization, to whom the Taliban offered official asylum, they could no longer defend their contradictory policies concerning the Taliban and discontinued negotiations.

Like Bin Laden, the Taliban did not approve of Western ways and culture. Unlike him, however, it did not have grandiose ideas of global jihad against all Western influence in the Middle East and Central Asia. As Afghanistan expert Peter Marsden says, "There was no concept of pan-Islam in the Taliban creed when they first came to power."[3] The Taliban's goal remained clear: to bring the entire country of Afghanistan under Islamic rule.

Less than a month after the September 11, 2001, terrorist attacks on the World Trade Center and the Pentagon, the United States and its allies began a bombing campaign and subsequent ground war against the Taliban because of its refusal to hand over Osama bin Laden, the suspected mastermind behind the attacks. Once again, the Afghan people found their homeland a very dangerous place to live. Many again fled to neighboring countries for asylum.

Within a few weeks, U.S. forces, along with a group of Afghan resistance fighters known as the Northern Alliance, had driven the Taliban from power. By 2002 plans were already under way to install a transitional government in Afghanistan. A *loya jirga*, or traditional grand council, was convened in June by the UN-installed interim authority and a group of tribal chieftains. Hamid Karzai, an ethnic Pashtun, was elected to head the transitional government.

As of spring 2004 Karzai's government had been only partially successful at unifying the country. Osama bin Laden remained at large, and the Taliban showed signs of resurgence throughout the war-ravaged country.

Notes

1. Ahmed Rashid, *Taliban: Militant Islam, Oil, and Fundamentalism in Central Asia.* New Haven, CT: Yale University Press, 2000, pp. 9–10.
2. Michael Renner, "Lessons of Afghanistan: Understanding the Conditions That Give Rise to Extremism," *World Watch*, March 2002, p. 36.
3. Peter Marsden, *The Taliban: War and Religion in Afghanistan.* New York: Zed Books, 2002, p. 71.

Chapter 1

Why the Taliban Rose to Power

1

The Unexpected
Rise of the Taliban

Peter Marsden

In the following excerpt, written prior to the Taliban's ouster
from power, Peter Marsden traces the quick rise of the Taliban
from 1994 to the time of the terrorist attack on America in
September 2001. Marsden describes how the group emerged
from obscurity to take control of most of Afghanistan, including the capital city of Kabul, by 1996. According to Marsden,
the Taliban's success can be attributed to several factors. The
group had the support of many displaced young men who had
been trained in the fundamentalist Islamic ideology the Taliban adhered to. In addition, the Taliban was able to obtain
large quantities of weapons with ease. Finally, as the group
swept across the country, it took on an almost supernatural
aura that discouraged the populace from offering significant
resistance. Marsden is the author of *The Taliban: War and Religion in Afghanistan*, from which this excerpt was taken.

It appears that the Taliban began as a small spontaneous
group in Kandahar, perhaps in early 1994. Its members,
who were described as religious students, are said to have felt
outrage at the behaviour of the Mujahidin [Islamic guerrilla]
leaders fighting for power in the city and to have decided to
take action to end what they saw as corrupt practices, drawing on Islam as a justification for their intervention.

How they moved from small group to major force is not
clear. However, it is thought likely that they were seen by el-

Peter Marsden, *The Taliban: War and Religion in Afghanistan*. New York: Zed Books,
Ltd., 2002. Copyright © 2002 by Peter Marsden. Reproduced by permission of the
publisher.

ements outside Afghanistan as being potentially useful in promoting their various interests, and that these elements decided it was worthwhile to provide them with some backing. The nature and extent of the backing received from outside has been the subject of much speculation. Pakistan, the USA and Saudi Arabia have all been implicated.

It is none the less clear that they benefited considerably from the willingness of young people, both from the rural areas and from refugee camps on the Pakistan border, to join their ranks as they advanced through southern Afghanistan. They were also able to draw on a significant quantity of weaponry, either abandoned by retreating forces or found in the process of disarming the population.

Ideologies Hard to Pin Down

The ideological underpinning of the movement has been a further cause for debate. There appears to be little doubt that the Islamic *madrasahs* [Islamic religious schools] in the refugee camps, where Islam has been taught on the basis of recitation of the Qur'an [or Koran], have proved to be fertile ground for recruits. It is also likely that the orphanages operated in the refugee camps, with funding from Saudi Arabia, the Gulf States and the Mujahidin parties, will have produced strong adherents to radical Islam, some of whom will have been attracted by the call to arms issued by the Taliban. Also evident is the role of the Islamist parties in Pakistan in training young people in their various educational establishments, and the contribution these establishments have made to the expansion of the Taliban movement. Equally unclear is the question of how the Taliban forces have received their military training.

There has also been much debate as to whether the movement is essentially a Pushtun [people of eastern and southern Afghanistan] one, given that an overhelming majority of its supporters have been Pushtun. This has led to speculation that the movement has been supported in an effort to reassert the Pushtun dominance in Afghanistan that existed before the war and was challenged by the control of Kabul by the Tajik leadership of [leader of the first Islamic political party in Kabul, Burhannudin] Rabbani and [another member of this political party, Ahmed Shah] Masoud. The Taliban have insisted that the movement is open to all ethnic groups in Afghanistan and it is clear that some of the adherents are, indeed, non-Pushtuns. The movement is, however, exclusively Sunni [an orthodox branch of Islam] in its interpretation of Islam and cannot, therefore, embrace the Shi'as [another branch of Islam] of central Afghanistan or the Ismailis [another branch of Islam] of the north-east.

The movement depends very heavily on the continued commitment of its footsoldiers, some of whom will have already seen friends martyr themselves for the cause.

The absolute leader of the Taliban is Mullah Muhammad Omar, who has been given the supreme religious title of Amir Al-Mu'minin (Leader of the Faithful). He presides over the Kandahar *shura* [meeting], which has authority over the *shuras* in other Taliban-controlled areas. Herat has a governor but Kabul is controlled by a six-man *shura*, presided over by the president of the *shura*, and by a number of government ministers. Decision-making within the Taliban is reported to be by consensus. There is, therefore, a tendency for more conservative elements to prevail.

Mullah Omar is a Pushtun from south-western Afghanistan. He was previously a member of one of the traditionalist Mujahidin parties, Hisb-e-Islami, headed by Younis Khalis. He acquired a reputation as a brilliant commander and lost an eye in fighting against the Soviet forces. He is said to be in his late thirties or early forties. An aura of mystery surrounds Mullah Omar, because he is rarely seen in public or by visiting dignitaries. He limits his contacts to a few close associates, including the governors he has appointed, and is said to give his time exclusively to the organisation of the Taliban's military campaign. He often leaves the tasks associated with relating to the outside world, including meetings with heads of state and the UN secretary-general's special envoy, to his subordinates. He is said to be pious and to live very simply.

Governing

The movement depends very heavily on the continued commitment of its footsoldiers, some of whom will have already seen friends martyr themselves for the cause. Particular care has to be taken not to move too far in the direction of liberal, urban or Western values, lest the footsoldiers feel that they have been betrayed and withdraw the support on which the drive to take the whole country relies.

The Taliban have little experience in running a government administration, nor did they see this as a priority when they took power. They have demonstrated enormous single-mindedness in focusing on the military campaign, on the eradication of corruption and on the achievement of law and order. The maintenance and strengthening of administrative structures have been very much secondary concerns.

The capture of Kabul has brought a new entity, known as the Department for the Promotion of Virtue and the Prevention of Vice, to prominence. These religious police have played an increasing role in enforcing the Taliban policies on the urban populations. However, their actions have often contravened the policies of other elements of the Taliban leadership, leading to confusion and to speculation as to a possible struggle between hardliners and relative moderates within the movement.

The Taliban Was a Surprise Force

The Taliban appeared to emerge out of nowhere when they first came to the world's notice in October 1994. Their arrival on the Afghan military scene coincided with an initiative by the government of Pakistan to dispatch a trade convoy through Afghanistan, via Kandahar and Herat, to Turkmenistan. As the convoy entered Afghanistan, travelling north from Quetta, it was attacked by an armed group. Immediately, another group came to the rescue and fought off the attackers. These were the Taliban.

After allowing the convoy to proceed, the Taliban moved on Kandahar and took the city with almost no resistance. Kandahar had witnessed virtual anarchy for the previous two years, as a number of Mujahidin groups fought for control. The Taliban were able to seize the faction leaders, killing some and imprisoning others. Having taken the city, they called on the population to surrender their weapons at a designated place and to cooperate with the new authorities in bringing peace to the area. The people duly complied.

The Taliban simultaneously announced that it was their mission to free Afghanistan of its existing corrupt leadership and to create a society that accorded with Islam. They issued decrees in which they required men to wear turbans, beards, short hair and *shalwar kameez* [robelike garments] and women to wear the *burqa*, a garment that covers the entire body, including the face. Men were strongly encouraged to pray five times a day, ideally in the mosque. Women were advised that it was their responsibility to bring up the next generation of Muslims. To this end, they were prohibited from working. It was also made clear that the education of girls would have to await the drawing up of an appropriate Islamic curriculum by religious scholars, and that this process could start only when the Taliban had control of the whole country. Other decrees banned music, games and any representation of the human or animal form. In order to enforce these bans, televisions and tapes were symbolically displayed in public places.

The remarkable success of the Taliban in bringing order to Kandahar earned them considerable popularity and this, building on popular superstition and combined with their distinctive white turbans and obvious religious fervour and purity, lent them an almost supernatural aura. When they moved westwards from Kandahar, their reputation had already travelled before them and they were able to clear the main road of armed groups and bandits with great ease. As they captured positions they seized abandoned weaponry, some of it left in great haste, and encouraged people to join the ranks of their fighters.

Over the winter of 1994–95, the Taliban were able to repeat this pattern many times over and, by February 1995, they were positioned on hilltops overlooking the southern suburbs of Kabul, having taken almost half of Afghanistan. . . .

The Fall of Herat

While the Taliban were endeavouring to take Kabul, there was also intense military activity in western Afghanistan. The city of Herat was . . . under the control of Ismail Khan, who was allied to the government. He had taken Herat Province in April 1992, when the Soviet-backed government had fallen, and had gradually increased his dominion or influence over the western provinces of Farah and Nimroz, to the south, and Badghis, to the north-west. When the Taliban moved west from Kandahar, they sought to take the entire road through Herat to the Turkmenistan border. However, their way was blocked at Shindand, about 120 km south of Herat, where there was a large military airbase. Ismail Khan's forces mined the approaches to the airbase in an effort to withstand the forward advance of the Taliban. They were succesful in holding off the attack, but had to contend with a wave of [Taliban] men willing to martyr themselves for the cause as they rushed forward over the minefields. This aspect of Taliban strategy added further to the image of invincibility that went before them. . . .

There has been much speculation as to why Ismail Khan gave in so easily to the Taliban and effectively handed over Herat to them. Rumours at the time that there had been differences between Ismail Khan and the central government in Kabul, which had led to Ismail Khan's resignation or dismissal from the post of governor, cannot be substantiated. Another rumour in circulation was that Ismail Khan wished to avoid the destruction of a city he had taken three years to rebuild and that he may not have felt able to count on the support of the population who, having enjoyed a period of peace, were reluctant to take up arms again. The fact that the Taliban had, up to that point, a reputation for behaving relatively well when taking new areas—they did not engage in looting, rape or mindless destruction—may have strengthened an assessment that resistance by the population on any scale could not be relied upon.

When the Taliban took Herat they issued edicts on the dress and behaviour of the population, as they had done in Kandahar, ordered the closure of all the girls' schools, and placed a ban on women working. The statue of a horse in the city centre was decapitated because, by representing the animal form, it was seen as being inconsistent with Islam. The Taliban conducted house-to-house searches to disarm the population.

The edicts relating to female access to education and employment had a greater impact than they had had in Kandahar. In Kandahar, the administrative infrastructure had effectively collapsed by the time the Taliban arrived and there were few girls' schools in operation. There were also very few opportunities for women to seek employment outside the home. However, in Herat city in 1994 there was a reported school population of 21,663 girls and 23,347 boys. By contrast, in the rural areas, 1,940 girls were attending school as compared with 74,620 boys. . . . A significant proportion of the teachers were women and it proved necessary to close many boys' schools as a result. Further, much of the population of Herat had lived as refugees in Iran, where female access to education had been provided as a right. The bans on girls being educated, pending the introduction of a new and more appropriate curriculum, and on women working, therefore had a significant impact.

Liberal Herat Suffers Under the Taliban

The capture of Herat by the Taliban was felt to be a military occupation, not only because of the restrictions placed on female access to education and employment but also because, culturally and linguistically, the predominantly Pushtun and rural Taliban were very different from the Persian-speaking Heratis, with their long aesthetic and liberal traditions.

During the early months of Taliban rule in Herat, long queues were reported outside the Iranian consulate as large numbers applied for visas for Iran. Many of these were educated professionals, a proportion of whom had been working in the various government ministries. There was an obvious slowing down in the construction sector, reducing the opportunities for people to engage in daily labouring work and accelerating the process of return to Iran. The repatriation programme from Iran to western Afghanistan ground to a standstill.

Humanitarian agencies sought to engage in dialogue with the Taliban in Herat as they had done in Kandahar. In the latter city, it had proved possible to secure authority for women to work in the health sector and this authority had been extended when the Taliban took Herat. However, the agencies in Herat were not able to achieve any modification of the ban on women working in non-health-related posts or a reversal of the closure of girls' schools.

Kabul Falls

Following the capture of Herat the Taliban made few gains until, a year later, they suddenly marched into Jalalabad, on 11 September 1996. Again, there was minimal resistance as the Mujahidin leaders who had composed the Nangarhar *shura* opted to leave without much of a fight. The Taliban then surprised all observers by forcing themselves through the apparently impenetrable Sarobi Gorge. After a few days of intense fighting in the eastern suburbs of Kabul, they walked into the capital on 26 September with scarcely a shot being fired. Shockwaves were then felt throughout the world when ex-President [Muhammad] Najibullah and his brother, who was visiting him, were seized from the protection of the UN compound, within a few hours of the Taliban entering the city, and hanged in a public place. It is still not known whether this hanging was authorised by the Taliban leadership or carried out spontaneously by enthusiastic followers, or whether others, with old scores to settle, took the opportunity created by the situation to wreak their revenge. . . . Others wondered whether Najibullah's years as head of the secret police had played a part.

The population of Kabul would, by this stage, have been apprehensive of a further prolonged siege of the capital. Many had already sold even their most basic possessions and were nearing destitution. When the Taliban entered there was therefore considerable relief and a hope that there might, at last, be peace and the possibility of an improvement in the local economy. It is likely that Rabbani and Masoud were aware of this view amongst the population, and this may have been a factor in their decision not to fight for every last inch of Kabul. The aura of invincibility held by the Taliban may have created an additional concern that the government forces would be unwilling to put up a fight. The government may also have calculated that opposition to the Taliban would grow once they had taken the capital, and Masoud made this view explicit in a number of subsequent statements. . . .

In Kabul, the Taliban proceeded to issue the same edicts as they had done in Kandahar and Herat. However, it soon became clear that there was to be a greater degree of enforcement of the Taliban requirements, particularly that men should pray at their local mosques rather than individually and that the dress codes for men and women, including long beards, *shalwar kameez* and turbans for men and the *burqa* for women, should be strictly observed.

There was also a downturn in the economy as there had been in Herat. This was in spite of easier access for trade than there had been during the previous siege of Kabul . . ., and in contrast to the mushrooming of the Kandahar economy during the post-Taliban period. In the case of Kabul, this may have been a consequence of many government servants suddenly losing their jobs or being paid only very irregularly when the Taliban took control. The departure, with the ousted government, of what little was left of the more affluent element of Kabul society may have accelerated this process. Certainly the Kabul money market, which provides a good indicator of the health of the economy, responded very positively to the Taliban takeover during the first week or so, but the afghani then fell in value again. . . .

Whether for economic reasons or fear of renewed conflict, there was a significant outward flow of people from Jalalabad and Kabul following the arrival of the Taliban. Ten thousand people left for Pakistan from Jalalabad in September 1996, some in direct response to a bombing raid launched by government forces. A further 50,000 fled to Pakistan from Kabul between October and December 1996 in response to Taliban restrictions and a growing climate of fear. Provision was made for the new arrivals at Nasir Bagh camp near Peshawar. As in Herat, this departure further weakened the government and reduced the pool of skilled professionals able to run an administration.

During the early months after the takeover of Kabul, the Taliban gave every indication of having overextended themselves. It proved difficult for outside organisations and diplomatic missions to be clear as to the nature of the internal decision-making process. There were inconsistencies in some of the public statements made, which created concern and confusion. Some of the soldiers in the streets appeared to be acting in the absence of any clear chain of command.

The Taliban Come Down Hard on Kabul

It was also evident that the Taliban regarded the population of Kabul as being very different from those living in other conquered areas. Many of them had their roots in rural traditions and gave the impression of seeing Kabul as corrupt and decadent. The behaviour of the footsoldiers at times reflected this attitude, and led to a number of incidents on which Amnesty International [an international human rights group] reported. The Taliban leadership gave every indication that they regretted these early excesses and Mullah Omar, the Taliban leader in Kandahar, issued an appeal on Radio Voice of Shari'a for his followers to treat the population of Kabul kindly.

There were also tensions in Kabul arising from Ahmed Shah Masoud's statements that he hoped the population would rise up against the Taliban. The Taliban were reported to have conducted house-to-house searches for those rumoured to be sympathetic to Masoud, and a number of people were arrested. Because of the absence of records as to who was held where, there was concern over apparent disappearances.

Three months after their capture of Kabul, the Taliban made another attempt to move north. This time they were successful in taking the settlements between Kabul and the Salang Pass, but they avoided some of the problems they had faced from insurrections during their earlier attempt by evacuating the area. Over a hundred thousand people were sent to Kabul as refugees while the Taliban consolidated their hold.

As 1997 took its course the numbers entering Kabul from the north rose gradually to 200,000. These had to fend largely for themselves, staying with relatives or finding some way of surviving. Appeals were made by the United Nations High Commissioner for Refugees for people to be allowed to return to their homes north of the capital, but these were rejected. The Taliban were totally focused on their objective of taking the whole country and did not want to take any risks. . . .

The Taliban Move North

From early August 1997, there were rumours of fragmentation within the ranks of the northern alliance [a group of militias opposed to the Taliban]. On 8 September the Taliban forces in Kunduz took advantage of a defection by a local commander in Tashkurgan, which sits astride the main Mazar to Pul-i-Khumri road, to launch an attack on Mazar airport. This coincided with a collapse of authority within Mazar as Abdul Malik departed and the city became parcelled up between Hisb-e-Wahdat, Jamiat [two Islamic political parties] and two opposing elements within the Uzbek camp, one affiliated to Abdul Malik [one of Dostam's generals who defected to the Taliban] and the other to the ousted [militia leader of northern Afghanistan] Rashid Dostam. However, the Hisb-e-Wahdat forces appeared to dominate the military scene and proceeded to loot the offices of humanitarian agencies, stripping them bare. When Dostam suddenly appeared in Afghanistan on 12 September, having made his way from Turkey, it was not at all clear whether he would be able to regain control of the situation. While he grouped his forces outside Mazar, the Taliban proceeded to encircle the city as September came to an end. However, somehow it proved possible for the northern forces to resist the Taliban attack and push the Taliban all the way back to Kunduz before the in-fighting between Abdul Malik and Dostam started again. The additional defeat increased the nervousness of the Taliban yet further, and they tightened their grip on the populations of Kabul and Herat. This further dampened economic activity as men became increasingly scared to venture out onto the streets.

It is almost certain that they killed large numbers of Hazaras.

In August 1998, the Taliban made another attempt on Mazar-i-Sharif, on this occasion facilitated by disunity within the ranks of the opposition. Their successful capture of the city was accompanied by a news blackout so that no journalists were able to witness or report what happened. However, from reports submitted by the UNHCR [United Nations High Commissioner for Refugees], Amnesty International and Human Rights Watch, and statements issued by the Iranian government, it is almost certain that they killed large numbers of Hazaras [a Shi'a population of central Afghanistan], possibly thousands, as an act of revenge for the Hazara uprising against them when they entered Mazar in May 1997 and the subsequent massacre of 2,000 Taliban prisoners by Abdul Malik's forces. In addition, eight Iranian diplomats and an Iranian journalist based in Mazar were killed. As the Taliban subsequently advanced on the Hazara stronghold of Bamyan the following month, the Taliban leader responded to concerns expressed by Amnesty International for the security of the Hazara population there by stating that he had ordered his soldiers to treat civilians and prisoners properly, thus acknowledging, implicitly, that they had not done so in Mazar. Reports were mixed as to how restrained the Taliban forces were in their successful capture of Bamyan on this occasion, but it is clear that the city has been reduced to rubble as the Taliban and Hisb-e-Wahdat have since fought for control of it and that both sides have had scant regard for the population affected by the conflict.

No further gains were made by the Taliban until September 2000, when they captured Taloqan in north-east Afghanistan, leading to the exodus of 170,000 people to Pakistan and the displacement of a further 80,000 within the area. They faced continuing resistance to their efforts to capture the remaining corner of the country, including the opening up of new fronts by the opposition in areas already under Taliban control. The Taliban were said to be facing increasing difficulties recruiting within Afghanistan and were resorting to forced recruitment, as were the opposition forces. Young men were reported to be making their way to Pakistan, Iran and beyond to escape such conscription. The Taliban were also accused by opposition forces of relying heavily on volunteers from Pakistani *madrasahs*, both Pakistanis and Afghan, and from other parts of the Islamic world. For whatever reason, the Taliban-led forces appeared to be behaving more punitively when they recovered territory lost to the opposition in the many clashes that occurred, often burning houses and bazaars. Of particular note was the massacre of more than one hundred civilians, reported on by the UN secretary-general and Amnesty International, which followed the temporary recapture of Yakawlang in central Afghanistan from Hisb-e-Wahdat in early January 2001. Also of note was the burning of the centre of Yakawlang some months later after a period of oscillating control.

The assassination of Ahmed Shah Masoud in early September 2001 might have been the precursor to a planned major offensive by the Taliban to capture the remaining area of the country under opposition control, in the north-east, but the terrorist attacks in the USA of September 11 will have diverted the attention of both the Taliban and their supporters to more urgent concerns and no such initiative has been taken.

2

The Taliban Offered a Peaceful and Moral Government

Ma'soum Afghani, interviewed by *Nida'ul Islam*

In 1997 the official spokesperson of the Taliban, Mula Ma'soum Afghani, defended the organization and answered its detractors. Downplaying any discussion of the Taliban's relationship with other Islamic groups, especially those in the Arab world, he said that the primary goal of the Taliban was simply to provide peace to Afghanistan by establishing sharia, or Islamic rule, throughout the country. In fact, most of the group's policies, such as confiscating the citizenry's weapons and ammunition and forcing women to abide by Islamic customs as the Taliban interpreted them, reflected this overall goal. Though foreign media reported the contrary, Ma'soum Afghani said the Afghani people had wholeheartedly supported the organization both financially and philosophically.

The official spokesperson of the Taliban Movement, Mula Ma'soum Afghani, denied any relationship with the Pakistani army, but he emphasised the keenness of the Movement to establish friendly relationship with all countries and parties. Ma'soum Afghani added in his talk with *Nida'ul Islam* [an Islamic magazine] that the Arab Mujahideen [Islamic warriors] who live in areas under Taliban control are "our guests", but they will not be allowed to use Afghanistan against other Islamic countries. He ascribed the Taliban

Ma'soum Afghani, "Our Goal Is to Restore Peace and Establish a Pure and Clean Islamic State in Afghanistan," *Nida'ul Islam*, April/May 1997.

strength to the anarchy and lack of security that over-whelmed the country during the rule of former Mujahidccn.

Ma'soum Afghani, the official spokesman of the Afghani Taliban Movement, in spite of his young age of 28, is con-sidered one of the founders of the Movement. He joined the Movement right from its emergence in September 1994 as a teacher at the national religious schools in Karachi [Pak-istan]. Because of his closeness to the decision making body, he was chosen as the first Taliban ambassador overseas. He is now in charge of the Afghani embassy in Pakistan. He led the Movement's negotiation delegation to Islamabad [a city in northeast Pakistan] for talks with the Uzbec [short for Uzbekistan, a predominantly Muslim country in west Cen-tral Asia] militia under the leadership of General Abdul Rashid Dustum, supervised by the United Nations. Like all Taliban leaders, Ma'soum Afgahni answered quietly, simply and in a fluent Arabic language the questions posed by *Nida'ul Islam*, which spread from history to present and the future.

Afghanis Support the Taliban

Nida'ul Islam: The Taliban Movement appeared in a short span of time and in special circumstances that raised a number of ques-tions and accusations against it. Would you shed some light on the Movement's ideology and thoughts toward the Islamic revival the-ory, its objectives, its source of finance and the identity of Mula Muhammad Omar and his group?

Mula Ma'soum Afghani: When the Jihad [holy war] leaders [those trying to maintain power prior to the Taliban rule] failed to achieve the goals and objectives of Jihad and were unable to establish an Islamic regime and State, anar-chy and lack of security and stability resulted. This in-creased with time in Kabul and elsewhere in Afghani cities. The Afghani people were subjected to the injustice of the Islamic leaders. The people had to face those actions, try to form the Islamic State and restore stability and peace in the country.

It is clear then that Taliban was supported and financed by the Afghani people and merchants. The Movement now controls 22 of the 30 Afghani provinces. It collects customs dues in those provinces, which provides a reasonable source of income to the Movement and its activities. Our goal is to restore peace and establish a pure and clean Islamic State in this country, which is the goal of every Muslim and religious student. Mula Mohammad Omar was publicly elected as the chief and *Amir-ul-Mu'mineen* (leader of the believers) and is now, with the grace of Allah, supported by the Afghani people. The merchants and businessmen also financially support us. *Amir-ul-Mu'mineen* now runs all the country's authorities and affairs. There is now a political consultation council for the Movement and a military consulting council for directing the battle. The ministries include: Pilgrimage, Trusts, Justice, Finance, Foreign Affairs, Culture, Migrants, Borders, Internal and other ministries.

Our goal is to restore peace and establish a pure and clean Islamic State in this country, which is the goal of every Muslim and religious student.

Can you tell us the role of the Movement's leadership in the Jihad against the Soviet invaders [of 1979–1989]?

Most of the Movement's leaders, headed by Mula Muhammad Omar, Ihsanullah, Wakil Ahmad Mutawakel and others participated in the Jihad. Before the Jihad, they were students in religious schools.

What is the nature of the relationship that links the Movement with the Pakistani army, the real ruler of Pakistan?

During the Jihad period, the scholars and students played a role in Jihad and in conveying the message of Islam. We do not have any ties with the Pakistani army because we aim for peace and implementation of Shari'a (Islamic Law) in our country. However, we want good relationships with Pakistan and with every Muslim country within the Islamic system and law.

Ties to Other Islamic Groups Denied

How do you evaluate your relationship with the Arab Mujahideen [primarily Osama bin Laden and his organization of al Qaeda] who are currently residing in Afghanistan? And what is the basis of the relationship?

This relationship is based on this: the Arabs fulfilled their role in Jihad in Afghanistan against Communism. We have relationships with some of them but not all of them are under our control or on our land. They live in Afghanistan as guests, but the land of Afghanistan will not be used against any other Islamic country.

Do you have any ties with other Islamic Movement in the world?

We are currently interested in restoring peace and stability and implementing Shari'a. We do not have time to establish relationships with other Islamic Movements in the world.

What are the basis and preconditions that direct Taliban in their negotiations with the warring parties to put an end to the Afghani war?

The political principles of the Movement are stability in Afghanistan, implementation of Shari'a, collecting weapons and ammunition and transferring them to major military bases. These weapons will be submitted to a responsible body. When collection of the weapons and ammunition in Afghanistan is completed, peace and stability will be restored. That is why there is no priority for negotiations under the threat of weapons. Taliban now controls 80% of the land in Afghanistan and implements Shari'a on it, and peace prevails there. Weapons and ammunition must be collected from those militias. When other groups failed in the past in achieving this goal, the need for their existence became unjustified. Those other groups must therefore submit what they have to Taliban and save their country from killing and destruction. They should not give a chance to external interference in Afghanistan. . . .

The Taliban Seeks Peaceful Interactions

What is the Movement's position regarding the aggressions of the United States against Islam and its attitude toward Taliban's implementation of Islam?

Islam is a comprehensive way of life. It contains Islamic fundamentals and principles. It teaches us good relationships with other parties whether they are Muslim or non-Muslim. These are the basics of Islam with which we must abide.

The Movement calls for implementing Islam. How will you achieve this politically, economically, militarily and socially?

Islam is a comprehensive way of life. It has radiating basics for every social, political, economical and military event. As far as women are concerned, they also must abide by the Islamic teachings and they will get all their rights granted by Islam. Under current circumstances, it is hard for us to provide education for women, due to our economical condition.

What is the Movement's position toward Russia, the recently independent Muslim republics ruled by Communists, and Iran?

We seek good relationships with every Islamic country. We want Iran to stop interfering in Afghanistan. If it does this, our relations will be good. We are working to establish good relationships with the others irrespective of their rulers.

Do you have a word to direct to the Muslims across Nida'ul Islam?

We want all nations, particularly in the Islamic world, to recognise the Islamic Government of Taliban. Muslims have struggled and supported us to achieve this goal, and it has been achieved. The students . . . have established this Government under the leadership of *Amir-ul-Mu'mineen*, the Mujahid Mula Muhammad Omar. Now it is the responsibility of the whole Islamic world to stand by and support this Government. We call upon all the scholars of the Islamic world to come and examine the Islamic Government of Taliban.

3

The Taliban Has Roots in Islamic Extremist Movements

Kamal Matinuddin

According to Kamal Matinuddin, Taliban expert and Afghani native, many of the men responsible for teaching the young men who would eventually form the Taliban held limited but hardly insignificant religious and political power in Afghanistan in the first half of the twentieth century. As early as the 1950s, these teachers established conservative and unaccredited religious schools along the border of Afghanistan, and their ideas were gradually welcomed by thousands of these male students, or Talibs, throughout the country. Funded by Islamic extremists in neighboring countries such as Saudi Arabia who applauded their religious and political views, this coalition of students, now the Taliban, began to take hold of Afghanistan when the country had reached a point of such political unrest that their strict religious views provided some promise of stability.

*T*alib is an Arabic word, the literal meaning of which is one who is seeking something for himself. It is derived from the word *talab*, meaning desire. In Urdu [official language of Pakistan] it is generally affixed with another word to clarify what is being sought, for example, *Talib-e-didar* (one who is seeking the sight of his beloved), *Talib-e-duniya* (one who seeks the pleasures of this world). Hence the Urdu

Kamal Matinuddin, *The Taliban Phenomenon: Afghanistan, 1994–1997*. Karachi, Pakistan: Oxford University Press, 1999. Copyright © 1999 by Oxford University Press. Reproduced by permission.

word *Talib-e-ilm* is a person in search of knowledge i.e., a student. *Taliban* is the plural of *talib*. In Pushto the word *taliban* generally denotes students studying in *deeni madaris* (religious institutions).

The *Deeni Madaris* Have Great Influence

Religious seminaries in Central Asia, Afghanistan, and in undivided India have played a significant role in the spiritual uplift of the Muslims in the South Asian region for centuries. Well-known institutions like the Firangi Mahal in Lucknow [India] and the *madaris* at Nadwa, Deoband, Bareilly, and Azamgarh (all in India) have produced luminaries who have served the interests of Muslims the world over. They were also, however, instrumental in dividing the *Ummah* [united Muslim world] into different schools of thought and in narrowing the vision of those who passed through their portals.

Deeni madaris are an offshoot of the old *madrassa* educational system. Some of these led to the formation of religious groups which adopted a very rigid attitude towards the implementation of what they believed to be true Islamic values. Quite a few young minds were brainwashed, by these religious groups into carrying forward the messianic spirit of Islam to other parts of the world. Their dogmatic approach and intolerance of others' points of view often produced fanatics who were recruited for trans-territorial missions.

A BBC [British Broadcasting Company] documentary screened in 1997 showed some students in chains in one of the *deeni madaris* being taught to memorize the verses of the Holy Koran. What was even more appalling was that the head of that particular institution defended this practice by saying that the chained *talibs* would otherwise run away to their homes.

The Taliban Draw on a Long History

Though the Taliban phenomenon is of recent origin, *talibs* appeared on the scene several decades ago. They used to go to different *aalims* (religious scholars) to acquire religious knowledge. But that did not prevent them from participating in tribal dances, for which they were well known. Dressed in colourful clothes, with their well-kept hair flowing below their ears, they became part of Afghan folklore.

Many of them rose to become religious teachers and political activists. Fazal Omar Mojeddedi and Sher Agha Naguib were both *talibs*. They were among the religious leaders who had become the foundations of power in Afghanistan between 1929 and 1953. Mullah Shor Bazar, an Afghan fighter famous for having kept the British at bay during the Third Anglo-Afghan war of 1919, was also a *talib*, as was Mir Waiz of Kandahar, who also fought against the foreign occupation of his country.

There were around 2,500 spiritual teachers and leaders enjoying a vital leadership role in the village and tribal society of Afghanistan before the failed attempt to introduce communist ideology in Afghanistan.

Soon after the Soviets sent their troops into Afghanistan in support of the communist regime in Kabul [in 1979], General Mohammad Ziaul Haq, the then President and Chief Martial Law Administrator of Pakistan, established a chain of *deeni madaris* along the Afghan-Pakistan border. He did so in order to create a belt of religiously oriented students who would assist the Afghan mujahideen to evict the Soviet forces from Afghanistan. Of course, it was also to satisfy the mullahs [prayer leaders] who he was building up as his own constituency for political ends.

Schools for the Taliban Become Plentiful

Soon *deeni madaris* began to sprout in almost all the major cities of the NWFP [northwest frontier province of Pakistan] and Balochistan [southwest Pakistan and southeast Iran]. Later they spread to Punjab [region in northwest India and Pakistan] and Sindh [region in southern Pakistan] as well. They were to be found in as far away places as Gilgit in the north and Karachi in the south. 'I have studied at a *madrassa* in Gujranwala,' said a Persian-speaking *talib*. A survey carried out by the Home Department of the government of Punjab in May 1997 revealed that in Rawalpindi [Pakistan] division alone there were a total of 169 *deeni madaris*, and that 17,533 *talibs* were on their rolls. Most of these schools were being used as hide-outs for terrorists attached to foreign mentors, says the report. . . .

Statistics compiled by Dr. Syed Sher Ali Shah of the *Khadim al Hadith al Nabvi*, Miran Shah, gave a figure of 30,000 students from various *madaris* who joined the Taliban movement.

In addition to receiving donations from local philanthropists, the *madaris* were reportedly given grants from Saudi Arabia, Kuwait, and some other friendly conservative Muslim countries. General Ziaul Haq had also authorized the district *zakat* committees to give them money regularly from their *zakat* funds [Islamic tax given to the poor]. The report of the Special Branch of the Punjab police indicated that 37.87 per cent of the 169 *madaris* received government aid.

After the fall of Dr. [Muhammad] Najibullah [president of Afghanistan 1989–1993], religious schools began refunctioning in Afghanistan as well, specially in the eastern provinces and in Herat.

Haji Abdul Qadeer, former governor of Nangarhar, gave a figure of about 2,000 students (*talibs*) in the *madaris* established in the four provinces bordering Pakistan. The students in these *deeni madaris* were a mixture of Afghans and Pakistanis, with the majority being Afghan nationals. According to Mullah Shahabuddin, the Consul General-Designate in Peshawar of the Taliban regime, around 80 per cent of the students were Afghans. The teaching staff were both Pakistanis and Afghans.

The *deeni madaris* which were functioning in Afghanistan before the Soviets entered the country were running classes from Class 1 to Class 12 and were attended by students of all ages. After the Soviet occupation, these seminaries moved to Pakistan and established themselves in all parts of the country.

Taliban Degrees Were Considered Inauthentic by Some

The syllabi of these schools included the learning of the Holy Koran by heart; *tajweed* (correct pronunciation of the Koranic verses); *tafseer* (interpretation of the Holy scriptures); *fiqah* (Islamic jurisprudence); *shariah* (Islamic Laws); *ahadis* (life and decisions of the Holy Prophet [Peace Be Upon Him]) on various issues brought before him by the faithful); *mantiq* (philosophy); *riazi* (mathematics) and *falakiat* (astronomy); *tabligh* (spreading the word of God) and a smattering of modern subjects. [Mullah] Shahabuddin claims that the subjects ranged from the *Baghdadi Quaida* to *Bokhari Sharif.*

Unlike the well-known religious schools of pre-partition India, which awarded proper degrees to their students, many of these seminaries only gave a nameless certificate at the end of their studies which was not recognized by any other institution or government department, neither in Pakistan nor elsewhere. Mufti Mohammad Masoom Afghani, Ambassador-Designate of the Taliban regime to Pakistan was a product of one such *madrassa* in Gulshan-e-Iqbal, Karachi.

A distinction must be made between a *talib* and a mullah. A *talib* is one who has not completed his studies at the seminaries and has yet to be given the honorific title of mullah. A mullah, on the other hand, has gone through the designated number of years in the *madaris* under different religious scholars. Only then is a proper *dastar bandi* [ceremony] carried out and the recipient entitled to carry the title of a mullah. This allows him to become an *imam*, *qari*, or *khatib* [prayer leaders] of a mosque. Many are absorbed as teachers at religious schools, while others become *qazis* and *muftis* [Muslim legal experts], which qualifies them to conduct religious rituals and act as local judges in villages and towns. If this distinction were to be strictly applied, many of those who call themselves mullah amongst the Taliban do not really qualify for this title as they are only half educated and are not fully conversant with the injunctions of Islam and the correct interpretations of the Holy Koran and the Sunna [body of Islamic customs].

The *Madaris* Taught Students to Fight

The *madaris* not only imparted religious education of sorts, but more than that, they organized the students into militant groups who would be prepared to use force to subdue their rivals. The Taliban were divided into two categories. The first category was prepared and organized to take part in the jihad [holy war]; the second confined themselves to their studies only.

The size of the schools varied from fifteen students studying in mosques to around 2,000 in proper boarding and lodging institutions. It is the larger of the two types that produced fighters who went into Afghanistan to evict the communists and later fought against those who they believed were not introducing an Islamic regime in their country.

Those selected to fight were associated with various Afghan factions in order to obtain arms. Initially trained in how to fire a rifle, they soon moved on to use machine guns and rockets. During the three months of holidays (*Ramzan*, *Shawal*, and *Zi Quad*), those above eighteen years of age took part in the jihad against the Soviets and returned to their studies thereafter although many of them were martyred, maimed, or injured. (Shahabuddin denied that military training was being imparted to the students in the *deeni madaris.*) 'After the fall of Najibullah the Taliban came back to the *madaris* and laid down their arms,' said the Consul-General. . . .

The Origins of the Taliban

The exact origin of the Taliban movement is . . . still shrouded in mystery. Although several articles have been written on this so-called 'mysterious army', no researched or authentic material has so far been published on the historical perspective of the Taliban movement. The most widely circulated theory is that the leadership of the Taliban emerged from amongst the disgruntled young Afghan refugees studying in the *deeni madaris* around Quetta and Peshawar (even Lahore and Gujranwala have been mentioned in this context by some journalists). Senior officials of the Government of Pakistan claimed ignorance about the presence in Pakistan of any *deeni madaris* where the Taliban might have received their early education, though there is ample proof that this was so.

Professor Ahmed Hasan Dani believes that the Taliban received their education at *deeni madaris* in Pakistan and were also being supported by elements in Pakistan. Dani claims that the young students were being prepared for jihad against those who it was felt, were not adhering to the moral code of Islam. That is why they reportedly developed a dislike for the existing Afghan groupings, which they blamed for bringing about much of the death and destruction in their homeland. They realized that the people were suffering because of the power struggle that was going on between their elders.

Civil Unrest Makes the Taliban Attractive

By the year 1992, the average citizen of Afghanistan was sick and tired of the civil war that had been raging for three years. Masoom Afghani said that around 50,000 Afghans were killed in the struggle for power between [engineer and Islamic school founder Gulbadin] Hikmetyar and [professor and Islamic school founder Burhanuddin] Rabbani. The people had lost faith in their leaders, who were making and breaking alliances overnight. They found none of them trustworthy as they were not fulfilling their promises. . . . Their bitterness towards the leadership was increasing as they saw no end to the wanton killings which were being perpetrated in their country. Near famine conditions were adding to the anger which was building up against the once 'revered' Afghan leadership.

Unlike the well-known religious schools of pre-partition India, which awarded proper degrees to their students, many of these seminaries [madrassas] only gave a nameless certificate.

The popularity of the Afghan mujahideen [ruling party following Soviet withdrawal], therefore, was decreasing with the passage of time. Not only had they been unable to bring about peace in their war-ravaged country, but what was worse was that many of them had begun to engage in unsocial activities. All of them were armed. Quite a few had turned into gangsters and were extracting money from shopkeepers and levying taxes on passenger vehicles passing through areas under their control. According to the BBC, as much as $400 was being taken from every truck driver carrying goods bound for the interior. Passengers were made to pay 100,000 Afghanis ($2 approximately). Even those carrying goods on bicycles were deprived of some of their precious earnings before being allowed to proceed further. There were seventy-one such check points between Chaman and Herat alone. One of the reasons for demanding money, in addition to personal greed, was that the fighters were no longer receiving regular pay from the leaders who had earlier recruited them. Many were even indulging in corruption, looting, drug trafficking, and rape.

The worst-affected area was around Kandahar, where lawlessness had spread to such an extent that shopkeepers could not keep their goods in their shops during the hours of darkness. They used to bring goods to sell by day and take them back to their houses at night as they feared that the would be looted by bandits if they were left unattended after sundown.

Commanders Nadir Jan, Saleh Mohammad, and Doro Khan had bases on the Kandahar-Herat road near Mullah

Omar's village. They were known to be abducting and raping women. In July 1994 Commander Mansoor, one of the fighters in the Ismatullah militia, kidnapped three women who were gang-raped and killed. This sent a wave of indignation through the locals in Kandahar. Stories were afloat of tank battles between commanders over the possession of handsome young boys. A marriage between two boys, celebrated with a great deal of jubilation in Kandahar, aroused bitter feelings among the students and teachers of the *deeni madaris.*

There was mismanagement everywhere and the existing mujahideeen leadership was either unwilling or unable to curb the rising trend of anarchy in Afghanistan. Chaotic conditions prevailed throughout the country at that time, with the sole exception of the six northern provinces 'governed' by the Uzbek [Uzbekistan] General, Abdul Rashid Dostum.

The statements of the Taliban leaders and the actions they have taken in the areas they control put them in the category of extremists.

Afghanistan had become a failed state, like Somalia, Rwanda, and Burundi [war-torn countries in Africa]. Although physical boundaries still existed and the country did indeed still have a flag, a national anthem, a government of sons, membership of the United Nations, and embassies abroad, the writ of the government-in-being was not running even inside the capital. Warlords and petty chieftains had taken over the country. There was an economic collapse. Rabbani had no money to pay his 'army'. Food convoys were being looted. Virtually no outside government was willing to do serious business with the regime, with the exception of a few. In the words of a very respectable senior citizen, there was *tawaiful muluki* or a kind of a free-for-all attitude prevailing throughout the country.

Disenchantment, to put it very mildly, with the rotten leadership of the Afghan mujahideen was gradually building up. The harmony that had existed between them during the Afghan jihad [against Soviet forces] had gone to pieces. The ordinary Afghan was looking for a 'messiah'. It did not require much effort therefore, by the Taliban to garner support for ending the fratricidal [brothers killing brothers] war and the anarchy which was prevailing in their land.

The Taliban Are Pitted Against the Mujahideen

The education which the Taliban were receiving in the *madaris* from semi-educated *maulvis* [religious teachers], however, converted them into religious fanatics. They were made to believe that none of the then Afghan leaders were sincere about the establishment of what they perceived to be a truly Islamic state in Afghanistan. They were told that the struggle between Rabbani and Hikmetyar and the others was more about grabbing power than an effort to introduce Islamic practices in accordance with their own interpretations of Islam. The blame for the pitiable condition in which the Afghans found themselves was placed at the doorsteps of the existing mujahideen factions.

The Taliban came to the conclusion that neither Dostum nor Ahmed Shah Masood, who was in control of Kabul, had shown any evidence of changing the social set-up to bring it in conformity with Koranic injunctions. Nor, for that matter, had the Hizb-e-Islami [Pakistan-based militant group] chief, who was in the forefront during the Afghan jihad, anything to show in this regard. His sole aim remained the ouster of his political rival and the holding of general elections, which was not enough to pacify the rising religious emotions of the Taliban.

Afghans have traditionally looked up to a tribal elder or a religious figure to solve their problems and so, when one such person came forward to lead them out of the morass, they followed him without any hesitation.

Mullah Mohammad Omar, a jihad veteran from the district of Maiwand just west of the city of Kandahar, who had fought against the Soviets in order to see a truly Islamic government in his country, was most disappointed with the events that followed the ouster of Dr Najibullah. He had come back to resume his studies at the Sang-i-Hisar Madrassa in Maiwand after handing over all the weapons and ammunition he possessed to Abdul Rasul Sayyaf. In late September 1994, however, he decided to give up his studies and work towards achieving the objective of bringing about peace by evicting the pro-communists in his country and introducing Islamic values in Afghanistan.

The Taliban Try to End Lawlessness

On 20 September 1994, a Herati family, while on its way to Kandahar from Herat, was stopped at a check point ninety kilometres short of Kandahar by local mujahideen bandits. The men and women were separated. The boys were taken away and molested. The girls were repeatedly raped until they became unconscious. Later all of them were killed and their bodies partially burnt. It was Mullah Omar (sometimes referred to as Mullah Mujahid) who was the first to arrive on the scene. He is reported to have gathered some *talibs* who helped him in collecting the bodies. These were washed and given a decent burial. He then gathered the students and pledged to start a campaign to get rid of such criminals.

Some days later, Omar went to a mosque in his village to gather support for his mission. The seven students who were studying there did not accept his invitation as they thought the task was too big for them. But he did not lose hope; he went to another mosque and this time he was joined by about fifteen *talibs*, but they said that they would work for him only on Fridays as they were not prepared to leave their studies. By nightfall, however, around fifty students had joined him. The story goes that one of them had had a dream in which he claimed that he had seen angels descending from heaven, which to him was an indication that by following Mullah Omar they were on the right path.

Omar apprised them of his objectives, but he also told them that he had neither money nor weapons to offer them. The next morning one Haji Bashar, son of Haji Isa Khan, a mujahid commander of Hizb-e-Islami (Yunus Khalis) opened up his armoury and gave Omar both weapons and vehicles. The Taliban movement had begun. The formal name given to the newly-created political faction was Tehreek-i-Islami-i-Taliban Afghanistan.

The immediate goals of the newly-formed organization were to: (1) disarm all rival militia, (2) fight against those who did not accept their request to give up weapons, (3) enforce Islamic laws in the areas they 'liberated', and (4) retain all areas the Taliban captured. . . .

The Taliban, like all other Afghans, possess not only physical courage and a capacity to withstand extreme hardship, they also have a strong belief in the verses of the Holy Koran which say that a man killed in a jihad becomes a *shaheed* [martyr] whose spirit immediately goes to heaven.

The Taliban can be divided into three categories: those who concentrate on religious studies alone and after taking their degrees in theology become *aalims* (religious teachers); the militants, who may or may not have completed their studies but are willing to take up arms against the anti-Taliban forces; and the followers of the various other political factions, ex-communists, and former members of the Afghan armed forces who changed their loyalties out of fear or conviction, or for monetary gains.

While the vast majority of Afghans are devout Muslims and to a large extent live their life in accordance with Islamic principles diluted with their code of Pushtunwali [the honor code of the Pushtun Afghan tribe] and their local culture, their views on the implementation of the shariah differ. They too have liberal, conservative and orthodox elements within themselves. Although some Afghan rulers did try to introduce radical reforms, including the abolition of the veil and the introduction of western dress for women, the deeply-rooted Islamic values and tribal traditions did not permit these changes. Nevertheless, many of the educated elite of Afghanistan would still like to have leaders with a modern and liberal outlook.

The statements of the Taliban leaders and the actions they have taken in the areas they control put them in the category of extremists. . . .

The Taliban are strong willed and very dedicated to the cause they have set out to accomplish. They lead a very simple and austere life and practice what they preach. Most of the ministers and government servants draw no salary and continue to live in their modest dwellings. 'A guest is not entertained by slaughtering the fatted sheep but by a loaf of dried bread and curry diluted with water,' said Anwarul Haq, Deputy Administrator of Darul Uloom Haqqania, who was the guest of Mullah Hassan, a member of the Central *Shoora* [place and procedure for arriving at decisions] in Kabul. Mullah Omar received visitors sitting on the ground in a small house in Kandahar. No distinction was noticed between the ruler and the ruled. All were equal in the eyes of the Taliban.

One positive action by the Taliban in the areas they occupied was the banning of drug trafficking. Drug addicts were to be arrested and a proper investigation made to reach the supplier, who was to be severely punished. This fact was reiterated by Mullah Mohammad Rabbani, Chairman of the Caretaker Council of Afghanistan, while giving his government's policy at the Extraordinary Session of the OIC [Organization of the Islamic Conference] held at Islamabad on 23 March 1997. However, directives on banning poppy cultivation were not implemented as that was the only source of revenue for many in Afghanistan. Mullah Rabbani also informed the members of the OIC that his government was giving due consideration to the need to revive the educational institutions. He is reported to have said, 'Despite having certain financial constraints we have re-established the Kabul university'. As far as the question of female education was concerned, Rabbani said that the Taliban leadership believed in compulsory education for all male and female Muslims, and that the state was determined to start special schools for women subject to the availability of finances and suitable conditions. . . .

Outside Support

Many amongst us were not prepared to believe that a group of young Afghan students living in Quetta would be able to organize a movement on such a large scale by themselves. After all, it was not an easy task for raw hands to implement the stupendous task of overthrowing an established regime, however motivated they might be and however weak the *de facto* government in Kabul appeared to be. They surely must have received the tacit approval of, and financial support and training from, some other agency. . . .

One thing is certain: that without an outside agency the Taliban by themselves did not have the ability to organize a full-fledged fighting force. The training needed to operate sophisticated military hardware and the logistics required to sustain a conflict for so long were surely beyond the capability of these new entrants to the battlefield. Supply of ammunition, provision of fuel and rations at far-off places, maintenance of aircraft and modern weaponry, all these need money, organizing ability, and an expertise which these raw hands did not possess. Granted, they were not fighting a regular war on the pattern of modern conflicts, but even guerrilla warfare requires logistical support and outside assistance for it to succeed.

What observers failed to realize initially was that the young students were soon joined by experienced hands who

had been fighting against the Soviets during the Afghan jihad. It is they who were helping in organizing the 'war effort'.

A central *shoora* had been established in Kandahar, with
Mullah Omar designated as the *Amirul Momineen* [Islamic
title, Commander of the Faithful]. The 'war effort,' and all
policies were being directed from his headquarters in Kandahar, which virtually became the capital of the Taliban-
controlled areas of Afghanistan. According to a UN official,
Mullah Omar remained in the background, and most of the
time mediators in the conflict had to content themselves with
meeting second stringers. Representatives of the Taliban frequently met UNHCR [United Nations High Commission
for Refugees] officials in Islamabad and negotiated on behalf
of their *shoora* as far as the administration of the twenty-two
provinces under their control was concerned. . . .

The Taliban, however, lacked a state structure. Ministries, departments, bureaucratic machinery, and an organized army or police force, which are symbols of modern
governments, were not initially functioning in Taliban-
controlled areas. The educated officials needed to run ministries had mostly fled the country, and filling their vacan-
cies was not a priority. The first task was to establish law and
order and to ward off threats from anti-Taliban forces. The
trappings of government were to come later.

In May 1997 the Taliban claimed that twenty ministries
had begun to function and that they were engaged in long-
and short-term development programmes. However, almost all of them existed on paper only, as the trained man-
power needed to run the affairs of state along modern lines
was absent.

4

The United States Initially Tolerated the Taliban

Benjamin Soskis

When the Taliban took control, the United States was initially hopeful that the Islamic regime could unite and govern civil war-torn Afghanistan. According to Benjamin Soskis, the United States had several compelling reasons to want the Taliban to succeed. For one, the United States wanted the Taliban in power because Pakistan, a longtime ally, sanctioned the Taliban as a government. Also, the United States hoped that the Taliban's hard-line policies would restore order and prevent the need for American intervention in future conflicts in the region. Finally, a stable Afghanistan would allow a U.S.-backed oil company to build a lucrative oil pipeline through the area. Eventually, the United States could no longer deny that the Taliban was a rogue regime that governed Afghanistan with repression and violence. Soskis is a Richard Hofstadter Fellow at Columbia University and a former assistant editor at the *New Republic*.

O n September 27, 1996, in a storm of dust and pickup trucks, the Taliban swept into Kabul, the culmination of an 18-month campaign for the city. And perhaps even more than the pro-government mujahedin [Islamic guerrilla] fighters, who had retreated under cover of darkness the night before, the [former president Bill] Clinton administration was caught off guard. Few U.S. officials had considered the Taliban capable of such a rapid and overwhelming victory, and those who did were largely ignored. A little over a week earlier the State Department official in charge of Afghanistan had drafted a memo suggesting that a Taliban takeover of Kabul was likely; it did not reach Secretary of State Warren Christopher in time.

So the Clinton administration scrambled to respond. Within a few days the State Department announced that they would send an envoy to meet with the Taliban to consider the establishment of diplomatic relations. Answering a question about the Taliban's dubious human rights record, especially their treatment of women, a State Department spokesman declared that the United States saw "nothing objectionable" in their strict application of Islamic law and suggested that there was "an indication . . . that they intend to respect the rights of all their citizens." Responding to a report that the Taliban had apprehended Afghanistan's former Communist president [Muhammad Najibullah], castrated him, and hung him—along with his brother—on a Kabul traffic post, the spokesman called the action "regrettable." (A few days later the State Department condemned the killing.)

Why did the United States tolerate a regime whose abhorrence seems, in retrospect, blindingly obvious?

There would be, of course, many more reasons for the United States to regret the Taliban's consolidation of power. But America's faith in the regime's reformability proved surprisingly resilient. While the United States never formally recognized the Taliban as Afghanistan's legitimate government, it made no concerted effort to oust them. Unlike Iran and Russia, the United States offered little assistance to the Northern Alliance [Afghani forces opposing the Taliban], which was trying to overthrow the Taliban from within. Nor, until relatively late in Bill Clinton's second term, did the United States pressure Pakistan, the Taliban's primary external sponsor, to withdraw its support.

Why did the United States tolerate a regime whose abhorrence seems, in retrospect, blindingly obvious? One generous answer is lack of reliable, on-the-ground intelligence about the Taliban. Another is hope—the United States wanted to believe the best about Afghanistan's new rulers, even when the evidence suggested something very different. But to a large extent, ignorance and hope were covers for a deeper motivation: convenience. Believing in the Taliban avoided a conflict with Pakistan, which the United States considered a key player in the region. It afforded potential economic opportunities—chief among them an oil pipeline project. Most importantly it meant the United States didn't have to devote diplomatic, financial, or military resources to a messy political situation in a far-off land. After all, what was the Taliban going to do to us?

The United States Blindly Trusted the Taliban

The starting point for U.S. policy vis-a-vis the Taliban was not so much support for the regime as support for any group that would unify the country after years of bloody civil war. As one U.S. official told the *Los Angeles Times* in October, mere weeks after the Taliban victory, "We're not choosing. These people walked into Kabul, and they are no more or less legitimate than those sitting there last week."

But, of course, it wasn't self-evident that unified Taliban rule was preferable to civil war, and so the United States had to make a case for Pax Taliban [Peace of the Taliban]. By November the State Department was calling for other nations to "engage with" the Taliban—but not necessarily recognize them—in the hope of moderating the regime's fundamentalism. And many in U.S. policy circles were considerably more optimistic than that. Bolstered by credible reports that the Taliban were cracking down on the rape, pillaging, and general criminality that characterized their predecessors, American officials argued that, as far as the Afghan people were concerned, life under the Taliban could hardly be worse—and might well be better. In this sense the Taliban's extreme fundamentalism actually worked to the group's favor, since it lent the regime the aura of virtuous religiosity. As Ahmed Rashid writes in *Taliban: Militant Islam, Oil and Fundamentalism in Central Asia*, "Some U.S. diplomats saw [the Taliban] as messianic do-gooders—like born-again Christians." As then Colorado Senator Hank Brown said in September 1996, "These fellows are deeply religious and strongly anti-Soviet."

Some U.S. diplomats described the Taliban as almost quaintly amicable. "You get to know them and you find they really have a great sense of humor," one State Department staffer told journalist Richard Mackenzie a few months before the Taliban entered Kabul. Others even managed to find in the Taliban a streak of cosmopolitanism: In one December 1996 briefing, Assistant Secretary of State for South Asian Affairs Robin Raphel made sure to mention that the Taliban were composed of "intelligentsia" and "former civil servants," among other seemingly reformed elements.

These were, to say the least, counterintuitive descriptions of a military movement composed chiefly of poor students from religious schools in western Pakistan peddling a dour, ultrarepressive vision of Islamic law. And yet the Taliban quickly figured out what the United States wanted to hear. At a news conference after their takeover of Kabul, a Taliban representative claimed the movement desired "friendly and good" relations with Washington, would crack down on the illegal drug trade, and would not export radical Islam. If the Taliban found terrorists, the Taliban declared, "we will punish them hard."

The Taliban Proves to Be a Repressive Regime

But Washington should have known better. At the very moment the Taliban were distancing themselves from international terrorism, they were reportedly accepting money from and sheltering Osama bin Laden—a man whom the U.S. State Department had, just a few months earlier, identified as "one of the most significant financial sponsors of Islamic extremist activities in the world." Meanwhile, journalists familiar with the regime were warning that the peaceable rhetoric was a sham: "They're expansionist," one reporter who had extensive contacts with the Taliban told *The Economist* that October. "They often talk of their desire to spread their beliefs to Pakistan, Central Asia, the Middle East." And, of course, there was the testimony from the Taliban's opponents. Says Harun Amin, Washington spokesman for the Northern Alliance, "At the time . . . I told them that the Taliban are not going to change; it's not in their nature, it's not in their beliefs, it's not in their tenets to change."

And the Taliban quickly proved such predictions correct. Previously the movement had hinted that its restrictions on women—on everything from attending school to leaving home without a male escort—were temporary and meant for the women's safety. But within one month of their victory in Kabul, the regime was adding new ones—like a prohibition on women using public bathhouses.

Nor did the Taliban ever show the sort of regard for international norms that could have intimated their eventual submission to them; on entering Kabul, the Taliban had dragged the former president from a UN compound, where he had been granted shelter for the past few years. Soon after, senior U.S. officials claimed that U.S. policy in Afghanistan was based on establishing "a broad coalition government." Yet the Taliban refused to participate in the convocation of all of the country's feuding ethnic groups— what the Afghans called the loya jirga. All its mujahedin opponents, the Taliban insisted, were corrupt and criminal. Says Julie Sirrs, a former Defense Intelligence Agency agent who specialized in Afghanistan, "There were some bad signs from pretty early on . . . that I think were just ignored because we had larger geopolitical reasons that we wanted to believe that they would be a good group."

Among those reasons was Pakistan. U.S. officials hoped our old cold war ally would balance Iranian and Russian influence in the region. And to some extent it did. But in the process Islamabad clouded Washington's appreciation of the Taliban's odiousness.

The United States Followed Pakistan's Lead

Pakistan had its own reasons for wanting the Taliban to succeed—among others a hope that Islamic radicalism would keep Afghan nationalism in check, thus defusing potential border disputes between the two countries. During Afghanistan's civil war, Pakistan had reportedly provided the Taliban with crucial artillery support and opened its borders so armed Afghan refugees and Pakistani students could replenish depleted Taliban troops. And once the Taliban secured control of the capital, Pakistan did everything it could to encourage the United States to recognize their rule. For example, as Rashid writes, after the fall of Kabul, Pakistani officials told journalists that the United States supported the Taliban—even though U.S. officials insisted otherwise. Throughout the early '90s, when a CIA case officer repeatedly asked permission to contact the Northern Alliance, the group that now represents the largest opposition to the Taliban, the Agency denied his request. As Reuel Gerecht wrote in *Middle East Quarterly*, "The Pakistanis loathed [Northern Alliance leader Ahmed Shah Massud] and no one wanted to irritate the Pakistanis." And, according to Gerecht, even when U.S. officials finally agreed to meet with Massud in 1998, it was largely to encourage him to reconcile with the Taliban.

Remarkably America kept deferring to Islamabad even after the Taliban began providing refuge to bin Laden in late 1996. As a December 1996 report on Afghanistan from the Congressional Research Service declared, "the United States is unwilling to isolate [the] Taliban because Pakistan, on which the United States has consistently relied to protect U.S. interests in Afghanistan, supports the group."

Oil Interests Lead to U.S. Support

Another major incentive for condoning the Taliban was the prospect of an oil pipeline stretching through Afghanistan—a pipeline that would tap the vast resources of the Caspian region [between Europe and Asia] while bypassing Iran. Industry experts believed the pipeline—being pushed by a U.S.-Saudi consortium led by the California-based Unocal—could begin pumping one million barrels of oil a day, a number that could grow to five million in a few years. Unocal representatives courted the Taliban assiduously, hiring a bevy of consultants, including Robert Oakley, a former ambassador to Pakistan; Zalmay Khalilzad, now President George W. Bush's adviser on Southwest Asia on the National Security Council; and Henry Kissinger [U.S. secretary of state from 1973 to 1977]. In addition, according to Richard Mackenzie, Unocal received regular briefings from the CIA (the company has disputed this). Unocal officials believed that if the Taliban could consolidate power, they could provide a sufficiently stable environment to begin laying down the pipeline.

And so one Unocal official told Reuters [news agency] that the Taliban's takeover of Kabul was a "very positive" development, which could lead to "stability and international recognition." (Soon after Unocal backtracked, claiming it was "fanatically neutral when it comes to politics.") The Clinton administration took a similar line. In April 1996 Assistant Secretary of State Raphel told reporters that a primary reason for the United States to promote "political stability" (in other words, to accede to the Taliban's military campaign) was to preserve "economic opportunities" in the region. She stressed that a pipeline could bring much-needed jobs to the blighted country.

In the end, of course, the pipeline was never built and America gradually admitted to itself the truth about the Taliban. In November 1997 Madeleine Albright [U.S. secretary of state from 1996 to 2000], during a visit to Pakistan, called the regime's treatment of women "despicable" and condemned "their general lack of respect for human dignity." President Clinton also got tougher, in part because the Taliban's mistreatment of women had become an important issue to many American feminists, including the first lady. But by then the Taliban had consolidated their rule and pushed their opponents to the fringes of the country.

Chapter 2

Life Under Taliban Rule

1

Women's Suffering Was Immense Under the Taliban

A. Widney Brown and Farhat Bokhari

During its time in power, the Taliban received international criticism for its mistreatment of women. In the following selection, written at the onset of the U.S. attack on Afghanistan in October 2001, A. Widney Brown and Farhat Bokhari describe the cruel treatment of women under the Taliban and supply firsthand accounts by women who experienced the abuse. The authors spent extensive time in Afghanistan conducting interviews and witnessing these problems firsthand. Though Brown and Bokhari admit the basic human rights of Afghan women had eroded over many decades of the country's history, they maintain that these rights, such as access to education, health care, and employment, were completely taken away from women under Taliban rule. Brown is the advocacy director of the Women's Rights Division of Human Rights Watch, an organization that monitors and reports on human rights around the world. Bokhari is a researcher with the Women's Rights Division.

Historically, a succession of different [Afghan] governments, regimes, and political factions have manipulated women's rights in pursuit of their own political agendas, and some of these have sought to strip Afghan women of their fundamental human rights, freedoms, and dignity. Afghan women have symbolized their families' and societies' honor, and this concept of honor has been a potent source of political mobilization and manipulation by various competing forces. In particular, the seclusion of women and strict control over their movement is central to this honor code that is inextricably tied to the conduct of women. Under the Taliban, this control has been institutionalized by various edicts governing all aspects of women's public and private lives, by severely restricting women's freedom of movement and association, and their access to education, healthcare, and employment. Women in the cities have been especially targeted and have borne the brunt of the zealous enforcement of these decrees by the [Taliban's] Religious Police. But women in rural areas have also been adversely affected.

> *Women living under Taliban rule report being in a constant state of fear.*

The Taliban edicts formally order the seclusion and segregation of women from men unrelated to them. Thus, women are effectively banished to the domestic sphere, and may not be seen in public unless they are almost totally concealed in a chadari or *burqa*[1] and then only when accompanied by a mahram (a close male relative). Furthermore, women must not wear clothes that are decorated, brightly colored, or form fitting, and women are not permitted to travel alone in a taxi. Even as regards access to health care, it is not only the structural consequences of continuing armed conflict, but the restrictions on women's movement, such as traveling with a mahram and wearing a veil in public, that severely constrain their ability to seek and receive medical treatment. The very same discriminatory edicts inhibit the ability of female health care professionals to carry out their work safely and effectively and limit the few opportunities for professional development that women doctors hope to achieve. Similarly, access to education for women and girls has been further aggravated by discriminatory policies that ban girls from all but elementary levels of education, and ban women teachers from working. The punishment for violating these codes is severe. Typically,

---

1. Chadari and *burqa* are garments that cover women from head to toe.

members of the Religious Police accost and may assault or imprison women who breach these restrictive requirements.

Women Were Beaten for the Slightest Offense

Women living under Taliban rule report being in a constant state of fear. The slightest infraction, real or perceived, of gender-specific norms or mores as expressed by Taliban edicts can and often does lead to summary beatings by the Religious Police. There is no defense or appeal. Punishment is immediate and harsh. The opinions, thoughts, expressions, resistance and very existence of women is effectively denied by the existing policies that seek to make Afghan women invisible, as the cases documented below illustrate.

Most women Human Rights Watch interviewed had either been beaten or had witnessed other women being beaten. Women are not just beaten for violations of the dress code. They are beaten if they travel without a mahram. A woman doctor who left Kabul in January 2001 recounted the risks she had taken simply to get to work at her hospital. She worked long shifts and so took her infant son, whom she was breastfeeding, with her to her work:

> My husband hailed a taxi to take my child and me to the hospital. Five minutes later, a Religious Police car stopped the taxi. He made me get out of the taxi. I was lucky my husband told the taxi driver I was a doctor. The taxi driver told the Taliban that he was taking me to the hospital. There were three Taliban. One of them beat the driver with a yellow cable that was pretty wide. I was scared. He asked me why the holes in my chadari were so big? Why are you alone in the taxi? I asked, "Are you going to beat me?" I put my child away in the car and told them, "Beat me, but do not hurt the child." He beat me. I hid my face. He hit me several times—on the back and arms. I had bruises.

Women reported being beaten for all manner of dress code infringement including wearing their chadari loosely, or wearing the wrong chadari; for wearing wide ankle trousers that revealed their ankles; for revealing their hands; for lifting the veil when they could not see; and for not wearing socks or for wearing the wrong type of socks. The Religious Police beat Shokeria Ahmed, a widow, because she lifted her veil to inspect some cloth before she purchased it from a shop in Kabul:

> In March 2001, on a Monday, I went to get some ma-
> terial for tailoring. I took a piece of cloth and some
> colored string for that cloth with me. I had to put up
> my chadari to compare the color because the shop was
> dark. The Taliban came and they beat both the shop-
> keeper and me. They beat us with a wire, made from
> rubber with a wooden handle and the rubber attached
> to the end of it. They said to me, "stupid, cover your
> face." No one helped because no one can.

Similarly, in another case, a woman from Kabul was
beaten for lifting her chadari to reveal her face:

> About nine months ago, I was in Kabul. I was sitting in
> the front seat of a car. It was in the Foroushgah area—
> in the bazaar. I had gone to buy some cloth for the
> children. It was too hot and I had lifted the chadari
> from my face. A Taliban came and hit me on the shoul-
> der. He hit me with a cable. It hurt a lot. I had a bruise.

Women Must Wear the Veil

Meena Akram, a forty-year-old teacher from Helmand who
had spent part of her life in Kandahar, the seat of Taliban
power, related how various political factions in Afghanistan
have sought to control women's external appearance, especially their use of the veil:

> Before the Taliban and *mujahidin* [Islamic soldiers who
> opposed the Soviet invasion of 1979–1989], we wore a
> small *chadar* even in school. During the mujahidin pe-
> riod we wore a chadar namaz [prayer shawl]—like in
> Iran—our faces were visible. Once the Taliban came,
> we had to wear the chadari. We consider this to be the
> imprisonment of women. We cannot go out of the
> house and we have no freedom. If one has no freedom,
> one has nothing. If something is not according to a
> person's wishes, then it's not life; it's a prison for them.

Even women doctors are not exempt from obeying the
dress code while they are carrying out surgery or other
medical work in hospitals. Amna Atmar, told Human Rights
Watch that female staff were required to wear a chadar
when performing surgery rather than the usual headwear

worn to protect patients from contamination. Dr. Atmar recalled an incident in late 2000 when the hospital administrator instructed her to wear the chadar while she was in the middle of an operation:

> How do you want to prevent hair from falling off with a chadar? This is a hygiene issue. One time, he [hospital administrator] came in. I had a hat on in the surgery room. He said, "Go wear a chadar." The other doctors and I insisted that I stay. We had a debate on Islam, but I didn't leave. Ten minutes of discussion. The patient was lying there unconscious. I had already opened him. We kept saying we have to operate.

Another woman doctor from Kabul described how she had been assaulted in 1998 when she traveled alone in a taxi to the hospital where she worked:

> The Religious Police chased my taxi, and when I got out in front of the hospital, they stopped me and asked why I was traveling alone. I said I was a doctor and had to go to work, but they said women of Kabul are just prostitutes and addicted to traveling in cars alone. I had to call my boss to identify me as an employee of the hospital, but my boss said he could not confirm who it was because I was wearing a chadari. The Taliban asked me to put up my veil, and once my boss identified me, they hit me with their wire on my head and injured my eye. It took fifteen to twenty days to heal.

Fearing Prison, Women Limit Their Movements

Some women were imprisoned as well as beaten for violating these edicts. Human Rights Watch interviewed one doctor who reported having treated three women who had been detained in *Dar-al-Tadib*, a women's detention center in Kabul. One, the doctor reported, had been beaten on the head for begging; another had been detained for wearing a wide ankle shalwar (trousers), and the third for taking a taxi without a mahram. The last of these was a twenty-five-year-old widow suffering from facial paralysis, who was worried that her deceased husband's family would not accept her back because the Taliban had detained her. The three women had been detained for between twenty and forty-five days when the doctor saw them.

A female manager of a clinic told Human Rights Watch of a woman patient whom the Taliban had detained. She had gone to a store to buy sweets for a guest but was stopped and questioned by Religious Police. When she became angry at their persistent questioning, they took her and her infant child to Dar-al-Tadib detention center. Her husband tried to find her, but when he was told that she had been arrested for insulting the Taliban, he divorced her. As a result, when she was released from prison, she had nowhere to go with her child and so arrived at the medical clinic to seek help.

Many women told Human Rights Watch how they had feared being beaten and had adjusted their behavior and routines to reduce the threat. Zhora Shah, a twenty-seven-year-old literature graduate, described how difficult she had found it to give up work and to stay at home: "If women are deprived like this—of work and education—they will all go crazy." But fear had made her very cautious. "I spent my days at home. I lived with my family. Shopping for food was difficult. The Taliban sometimes beat up women where we shopped. My brother did most of the shopping. When I went out, I was very careful and did not go far." Another woman acknowledged that after years of seeing the Religious Police beat women for the most minor infractions, the threat was enough to ensure conformity: "Now there is less beating. People have understood and do not do anything to be beaten."

Khalida Parveen, a thirty-year-old mother of three who moved to the Saidabad neighborhood of Mazar-i-Sharif in 1997, after the mujahidin looted her house, told Human Rights Watch that after the Taliban takeover, she had rarely left her home:

> I stayed home. I only went to the bazaar with a chadari and came back fast. We were scared to look around. We heard that women were beaten for having their hand out or for having nail polish. People live in fear. If one is punished, everybody fears being the next.

Urban Women Suffer Greater Risk

Women from the cities, such as Kabul, Herat, and Kandahar, complained that these restrictions seriously affected their daily lives and caused them a great deal of stress. One

Afghan man well informed about the conditions and their impact on women in Afghanistan said that for many, the restrictions are so great as to render them house-bound and cause them to become extremely depressed, as there is nothing other than house work to occupy their time: "no television, no music, or videos. They have lost hope. . . . They are oppressed by laws, by the state, and by the family."

Many urban-based women have a pervasive fear of the Religious Police, having either been victims of their violence or having witnessed it. This fear further restricts their movements, forcing them to make arrangements to avoid leaving the home or traveling alone and to ensure that if they go out, they are accompanied either by their young sons, brothers, or a group of women. For those women who do have a level of mobility because of their work as health care professionals, the challenge is in dealing with the rules governing such limited mobility. One Kabul doctor, who had fled Afghanistan six months earlier, spoke of the problems she had faced:

Human Rights Watch encountered widespread fear and rumors of the abduction, forced marriage, and rape of women by Taliban forces.

We had problems less in the hospital than in our daily life. Going shopping, for example, was a problem. That is why my younger brother had to stay behind. He was fourteen, and when my parents left, he wanted to flee to Pakistan with them. But, if he had, I would have been unable to move around.

The general decrees controlling women's mobility also impair women's ability to access medical treatment. Women who must travel to seek medical attention may have to put off a visit to a clinic if they have no mahram who can accompany them. Even those women who do have a mahram may be reluctant to ask him to take time off from work to make the trip. In emergencies, this can prove too difficult to organize. Majida Akbar, a seventeen-year-old from Kabul whose sister-in-law went into labor on April 2001, stated:

We could not take her to the hospital. It was one hour

away by car. We were scared to take a taxi alone, and the taxi driver would not even take us. No one helped us. There were two old grandmothers who helped. Even the mid-wife cannot come out alone to help.

My other sister-in-law was in labor four months ago too. She also had to give birth at home. She bled a lot. We had to wait for the men to come to get the medicine to stop the bleeding. The baby came at 1:00 P.M. The bleeding started at around 2:30 P.M., and we received the medicine at about 7 or 7:30 P.M. The children were born ten days apart. . . .

Taliban Curtail Women's Rights to Work

Widows are also exempt from the edict banning work for women outside of the home. However, the approximately 40,000 widows of Kabul are destitute and unable to secure stable employment that would sustain them and their families. They also face continual harassment and violence by the Religious police. Rural women, though not exempt from the Taliban's discriminatory policies, tend to suffer fewer work-related restrictions because of the nature of their occupations. Many of the rural women Human Rights Watch interviewed worked actively on family farms or had been involved in home-based wool spinning and carpet weaving. Even when working from their own homes, however, as Taliban edicts permit, women were not safe from harassment by the Religious Police, especially in the more vigilantly policed city of Kabul.

An educated widow, Zafia Akil, who left Kabul in June 2001, explained the difficulties she had faced in tailoring women's clothes from her home. Apart from the problems of having to travel without a mahram and the difficulty of inspecting the materials she needed to buy for her work while wearing the chadari, the suspicion with which the Religious Police viewed her work was a further threatening impediment:

> The Taliban asked my customers, "Why are you going to her house. Are you going to gather and make plans against us?" I had a board outside which read, "Tailoring for women and children." Three times they came and warned me, and I told them, "I am a widow, what should I do?" The third time they took my board down and said that if I do not stop this work they will

kill me. They accused me of making plans against the Taliban. They said, "Everyone should sew their own clothes; our wives sew their own clothes. God will assist you, if you do everything as God wishes." It was the Religious Police, and I was forced to close four months ago and leave for Pakistan.

Women in the cities who lost their livelihoods as a result of the Taliban's edicts banning women from working attempted to find alternative means of generating some income for their families. One female refugee who had left Afghanistan two years previously described how she and other women had sought to survive:

> I worked in the radio. We were sent home. After two or three months, some women complained that they couldn't survive. So the Taliban said you may come and collect your salary. They did this until 1999. I stayed home, as everyone else I knew did. Women mostly were sewing at home for their survival. Later, even that didn't work because there was no market for what they sewed. . . .

Ethnic Minorities Are a Favorite Taliban Target

The Taliban has not only targeted educated, urban women for violence, but also women belonging to ethnic minorities, such as Hazara women. One thirty-five-year-old woman from Mazar-i-Sharif spoke of the deep fear among Hazara women of having their daughters abducted and raped by Taliban forces. This, she said, caused families to be eager to have their daughters marry. She said, "We are Hazaras and if there is war, they [the daughters] will be at risk of being dishonored." Another woman who formerly lived in Ali Chapan, a Hazara neighborhood, and had witnessed the Taliban capture of Mazar-i-Sharif in August 1998, said many Hazara families had hidden their daughters to protect them:

> We knew that if the Taliban came they would kidnap our daughters, and so we sent them to safe places. I sent my daughters to my sister's house, in the Tajik neighborhood away from the Hazara area. The aim of the Taliban was to attack Hazara places, not the Tajik areas of the city.

Rural Uzbek and Hazara women, who had recently fled

conflict zones from areas in the north of Afghanistan, re-counted that when the Taliban took over their areas, women, in particular, were ordered to stay indoors. Many rural women complained that while their freedom of move-ment was already limited by local custom and family prac-tices, the Taliban's orders had been even more restrictive.

Zhora Gul, a Tajik woman from Shomali, was forced from her home when the Taliban invaded her village some-time between September and December 1999. She told us that when the women in her family were escaping they lost their chadaries, which made them feel extremely vulnerable:

> When we were escaping, we lost our chadaries in the burning of the houses and had to wear only a chadar. When we traveled from village to village, the Taliban tore our chadars away in order to see if we were men or women. But, I think it was because they wanted to know if the women were young and beautiful. They took the young girls for themselves.

The following eyewitness testimony from a Tajik woman about the abduction of a number of women from the Shomali plains is representative of what many other women mentioned, but had not witnessed, and that human rights monitors have documented as having occurred in July–August 1999. The whereabouts of these women re-main unknown:

> About nine months or a year ago the Taliban came to Shomali. They told us to leave our homes. Then they set our homes on fire and forced us to sit in their vehi-cles. They brought us to the Russian embassy in Kabul. We are in favor of Massoud, and this is why they at-tacked us. At night we reached Jalalabad, where they separated us in different cars. I think about ten or fif-teen young women were separated from their families and put into other cars. The Taliban were saying that you are all going to the same place together with your families. The men, women, and children were crying, and shouting, saying why are you separating us and where are you taking us. There were too many Taliban, and a hundred families. There were a lot of cars and no one could disobey their command. They beat the men up with their guns; people did not know what was go-ing on because they were all being beaten. They took

us to the Russian embassy in Kabul, and we did not see the young women who were separated from us.

Human Rights Watch encountered widespread fear and rumors of the abduction, forced marriage, and rape of women by Taliban forces, but individual cases were particularly difficult to document. One important reason for this is the shame felt both by a victim and her family, and the victim's fears that her family and community may ostracize her as a woman who is raped and is perceived to have brought dishonor upon her family. Layla Shah, a twenty-year-old Hazara woman, still remembers what happened to her neighbor in Mazar-i-Sharif:

> Two Taliban did bad things to her. Now she has a bad name. She came to tell me herself. She was twenty-years-old. She is still there. She has a bad name and no one will marry her. She told me that they came to search the house and she was alone. That was the first time when the Taliban took over Mazar. They did not tell her anything. They just raped her. She said she screamed but they did not say anything.

2

Taliban Decrees Concerning Women and Cultural Conduct

Amr Bil Maruf and Nai Az Munkar

The following list of decrees imposed upon the people of Afghanistan by the Taliban's religious police is representative of the kinds of restrictions endured after the Taliban's takeover of the country. Taking or displaying photographs, public clothes washing, playing or listening to music, and nearly every other aspect of what most Afghanis considered morally neutral behavior was either strictly monitored or forbidden. For example, the closing of the women's bathhouses meant women no longer had access to hot water. Also, even though one ethnic group of men, the Hazaras, traditionally have limited beard growth, they were expected to grow a full beard in just six weeks to comply with Taliban rules. To complain or rebel in any way against these edicts meant punishment.

(This translation from Dari [one of the languages used in Afghanistan] was handed to Western agencies to implement; the grammar and spellings are reproduced here as they appeared in the original.)

Instructions for Women

Decree announced by the General Presidency of Amr Bil Maruf and Nai Az Munkar (Religious Police).
   Kabul, November 1996.

Amr Bil Maruf and Nai Az Munkar, Taliban decree relating to women and other cultural issues, November/December 1996.

Women you should not step outside your residence. If you go outside the house you should not be like women who used to go with fashionable clothes wearing much cosmetics and appearing in front of every men before the coming of Islam.

Islam as a rescuing religion has determined specific dignity for women, Islam has valuable instructions for women. Women should not create such opportunity to attract the attention of useless people who will not look at them with a good eye. Women have the responsibility as a teacher or coordinator for her family. Husband, brother, father have the responsibility for providing the family with the necessary life requirements (food, clothes etc.). In case women are required to go outside the residence for the purposes of education, social needs or social services they should cover themselves in accordance with Islamic Sharia regulation. If women are going outside with fashionable, ornamental, tight and charming clothes to show themselves, they will be cursed by the Islamic Sharia and should never expect to go to heaven.

After one and a half months, if anyone observed has shaved and/or cut his beard, they should be arrested and imprisoned until their beard gets bushy.

All family elders and every Muslim have responsibility in this respect. We request all family elders to keep tight control over their families and avoid these problems. Otherwise these women will be threatened, investigated and severely punished as well as the family elders by the forces of the Religious Police (*Munkrat*).

The Religious Police have the responsibility and duty to struggle against these social problems and will continue their effort until evil is finished.

Rules for Hospitals and Clinics

Rules of work for the State Hospitals and private clinics based on Islamic Sharia principles. Ministry of Health, on behalf of Amir ul Momineen Mullah Mohammed Omar. Kabul, November 1996.

1. Female patients should go to female physicians. In

case a male physician is needed, the female patient should be accompanied by her close relative.

2. During examination, the female patients and male physicians both should be dressed with Islamic *hijab* (veil).

3. Male physicians should not touch or see the other parts of female patients except for the affected part.

4. Waiting room for female patients should be safely covered.

5. The person who regulates turn for female patients should be a female.

6. During the night duty, in what rooms which female patients are hospitalized, the male doctor without the call of the patient is not allowed to enter the room.

7. Sitting and speaking between male and female doctors are not allowed, if there be need for discussion, it should be done with *hijab*.

8. Female doctors should wear simple clothes, they are not allowed to wear stylish clothes or use cosmetics or make-up.

9. Female doctors and nurses are not allowed to enter the rooms where male patients are hospitalised.

10. Hospital staff should pray in mosques on time.

11. The Religious Police are allowed to go for control at any time and nobody can prevent them.

Anybody who violates the order will be punished as per Islamic regulations.

Guidelines for Punishment

General Presidency of Amr Bil Maruf. Kabul, December 1996.

1. To prevent sedition and female uncovers (Be Hejabi). No drivers are allowed to pick up women who are using Iranian *burqa*. In case of violation the driver will be imprisoned. If such kind of female are observed in the street their house will be found and their husband punished. If the women use stimulating and attractive cloth and there is no accompany of close male relative with them, the drivers should not pick them up.

2. To prevent music. To be broadcasted by the public information resources. In shops, hotels, vehicles and rickshaws cassettes and music are prohibited. This matter should be monitored within five days. If any music cassette found in a shop, the shopkeeper should be imprisoned and the shop

locked. If five people guarantee the shop should be opened the criminal released later. If cassette found in the vehicle, the vehicle and the driver will be imprisoned. If five people guarantee the vehicle will be released and the criminal released later.

3. To prevent beard shaving and its cutting. After one and a half months, if anyone observed has shaved and/or cut his beard, they should be arrested and imprisoned until their beard gets bushy.

4. To prevent keeping pigeons and playing with birds. Within ten days this habit/hobby should stop. After ten days this should be monitored and the pigeons and any other playing birds should be killed.

5. To prevent kite-flying. The kite shops in the city should be abolished.

6. To prevent idolatory. In vehicles, shops, hotels, room and any other place pictures/portraits should be abolished. The monitors should tear up all pictures in the above places.

7. To prevent gambling. In collaboration with the security police the main centres should be found and the gamblers imprisoned for one month.

8. To eradicate the use of addiction. Addicts should be imprisoned and investigation made to find the supplier and the shop. The shop should be locked and the owner and user should be imprisoned and punished.

9. To prevent the British and American hairstyle. People with long hair should be arrested and taken to the Religious Police department to shave their hair. The criminal has to pay the barber.

10. To prevent interest on loans, charge on changing small denomination notes and charge on money orders. All money exchangers should be informed that the above three types of exchanging the money should be prohibited. In case of violation criminals will be imprisoned for a long time.

11. To prevent washing cloth by young ladies along the water streams in the city. Violator ladies should be picked up with respectful Islamic manner, taken to their houses and their husbands severely punished.

12. To prevent music and dances in wedding parties. In the case of violation the head of the family will be arrested and punished.

13. To prevent the playing of music drum. The prohibition of this should be announced. If anybody does this then

the religious elders can decide about it.

14. To prevent sewing ladies cloth and taking female body measures by tailor. If women or fashion magazines are seen in the shop the tailor should be imprisoned.

15. To prevent sorcery. All the related books should be burnt and the magician should be imprisoned until his repentance.

16. To prevent not praying and order gathering pray at the bazaar. Prayer should be done on their due times in all districts. Transportation should be strictly prohibited and all people are obliged to go to the mosque. If young people are seen in the shops they will be immediately imprisoned.

3

The Taliban Imposed Order in Afghanistan

Sayyid Rahmatullah Hashemi

In a speech delivered months before the September 11, 2001, terrorist attacks, Taliban ambassador Sayyid Rahmatullah Hashemi defended the organization and its seemingly harsh policies as the only stabilizing force Afghanistan had seen in decades of civil unrest. He maintained that the Taliban had reunified the country, primarily by disarming the civilian population of the guns they had received during the Soviet occupation in the 1980s. Along with uniting the country, Hashemi said that the Taliban had restored human rights and halted the country's opium trade. Hashemi placed the blame for Afghanistan's problems at the feet of other nations, such as the United States and Russia, who had used the country as a pawn in a battle for political and economic control of a crucial geographic region.

The problem of Afghanistan [is] not new. As you know that Afghanistan is called the Crossroads of Asia. So, we are suffering because of our geo-strategic location. We have suffered in the 18th century, 19th century, and we are still suffering in this century.

We have not attacked the British. We have not attacked the Russians. It was them who attacked us. So the problems in Afghanistan, you see [are] not our creation. That reflects the image of the world. If you don't like the image in the mirror, do not break the mirror; break your face.

Sayyid Rahmatullah Hashemi, speech given at the University of Southern California, March 10, 2001.

The problems in Afghanistan started in 1979. Afghanistan was a peaceful country and it was doing its own job. The Russians, along with their 140,000 troops, attacked Afghanistan in December of 1979, just 21 years ago, stayed there for a decade, killed one and a half million people, maimed one million more people, and six million out of the eighteen million people migrated because of the Russian brutalities. Even today, our children are dying because of the landmines that they planted for us. And nobody knows about this.

After the Russians left during the Russian occupation, on the other side, the American government, the British government, the French, the Chinese, and all of the rest, supported the counter-revolutionaries called the Mujahideen; 7 parties only in Pakistan and 8 parties in Iran who fought the Russian occupation. And after the Russians left, these parties went into Afghanistan. All of them had different ideologies, a lot of weapon[s]. And instead of having a single administration, they fought in Afghanistan. The destruction that they brought was worse than the destruction the Russians brought. 63,000 people were killed only in the capitol, Kabul. . . . And after the Soviets left, another million people migrated because of the lawlessness that existed in Afghanistan. . . .

They are terrorist states; we are not.

So seeing this destruction and lawlessness, a group of students called the Taliban—Taliban is the plural word of students in our language; it may be two students in Arabic, but in our language it means students—so a group of students started a movement called the Movement of Students. It first started in a village in the southern province of Afghanistan, called Kandahar. It happened when a warlord, or a commander abducted two minor girls, raped them, and the parents of those girls went to a school and asked the teacher of the school to help them. The teacher of that school, along with his 53 students, finding only 16 guns, went and attacked the base of that commander. After releasing those two girls, they hanged that commander, and so many of their [the commander's] people were also hanged. This story was told everywhere; and this was called the terrorist story of the Taliban, or the Students. BBC [British

Broadcasting Company] also quoted this story. Seeing or hearing this story, many other students joined this movement and started disarming the rest of the warlords, who were worse than these. I will not prolong this story so far: This same students movement controls 95% of the country; they captured the capitol, including the four major cities. And only a bunch of those warlords are remaining in the northern corridor of Afghanistan.

The Taliban's Achievements

So our achievements are as follows. We are in a government for only five years, and the following things that we have done, and many of you may not know:

The first thing we have done is reunify the fragmented country. Afghanistan was formerly fragmented into five parts. The first thing we have done is to reunify that country. The United Nations, the United States, everybody was confused as to how to reunify that country, and nobody could do it. First thing we have done is to reunify that country. Second thing we have done, which everybody failed to do, was disarming a population. After dealing [with] the war of the Russians, and the Americans I would say, every Afghan got a Kalashnikov, and even sophisticated weapons such as stinger missiles, and they even got fighter planes and fighter helicopters. So disarming these people was impossible. The United Nations in 1992 passed an appeal asking for 3 billion dollars to re-purchase [those] arms, to start a process of repurchasing those arms. And suddenly, because of its impracticability, that plan never materialized, and everybody forgot about Afghanistan. So the second thing we have done is to disarm 95% of that country. And the third thing that we have done is to establish a single administration under Afghanistan, which did not exist for 10 years. And the fourth achievement that we have that is surprising to everybody is that we have eradicated 75% of all [the] world's opium cultivation. Afghanistan produced 75% of all [the] world's opium. . . . And last year we issued an edict asking the people to stop growing opium, and this year, the United Nations Drug Control Program, UNDCP, and their head, [Mr.] Barnard F., proudly announced that there was 0% of opium cultivation. . . . And this was not good news for UN itself because many of them lost their jobs. In the UNDCP, 700 so-called experts were working there and they got their salaries and they never went into Afghanistan. So when we issued this edict, I know that they were not happy. And this year they lost their jobs. And this was our fourth achievement.

The Restoration of Human Rights

The fifth achievement . . . is the restoration of human rights. Now, You may think that is a violation of human rights, but from our perspective that is the restoration of human rights. Because usually [among] the fundamental rights of a human being is the right to live.

Before us, nobody could live peacefully in Afghanistan. So the first thing we have done, begun [to give] to the people is a secure and peaceful life. The second major thing that we have restored is to give them free and fair justice; you don't have to buy justice, unlike here. You will have justice freely. And you have criticized us for violating women's rights; now, who knows what happened before us? Only some symbolic schools or symbolic posts were given to some women in the ministry, and that was called the restoration of women's rights.

I can see some Afghans living here, and they will agree with me that in the rural areas of Afghanistan, women were used as animals. They were sold actually. The first thing we have done is to give the self-determination to women, and it happened not in the history of Afghanistan. Throughout the history of Afghanistan, during all the so-called civilized kings or whatever, they didn't give this right to women, so women were sold! They didn't have the right to select their husbands or to reject their husbands. First thing we have done is to let them choose their future. And you will know that through-out south Asia women are killed under the title of honor killings. It happens when a woman's relation is detected with a man, whether or not the relation was sexual, they're both killed. But now this is not happening in our country.

Restoring Women's Rights Will Take Time

And the third thing that happened only in Afghanistan was women were exchanged as gifts; this was not something re-ligious; this was something cultural. When two tribal tribes were fighting among themselves, then in order to get their tribal issue reconciled, they would exchange women, and then [they] would make or announce reconciliation. And this has been stopped. If we [had to give] fundamental rights to women, we had to start from zero; we couldn't jump in the middle.

Now you've asked me about the rights of women's education and the rights of women's work. Unlike what is said here, women do work in Afghanistan. You're right that . . . in 1996 when we captured the capitol Kabul we did ask women to stay home. It didn't mean that we wanted them to stay at home forever, but nobody listened to us. We said that there is no law, and there is no order, and [they] have to stay at home. They were raped before us every day. So, after we disarmed the people, and after we brought law and order, and now women are working.

You are right that women are not working in the ministry of defense, like here. We don't want our women to be fighter pilot[s], or to be used as objects of decoration for advertisements. But they do work. They work in the Ministry of Health, Interior, Ministry of Education, Ministry of Social Affairs, and so on. . . . And we don't have any problem with women's education. We have said that we want education, and we will have education whether or not we are under anybody's pressure, because that is part of our belief. We are ordered to do that. When we say that there should be segregated schools, it does not mean that we don't want our women to be educated.

Taliban Are Against Co-education

It is true that we are against co-education; but it is not true that we are against women's education. We do have schools even now, but the problem is the resources. We cannot expand these programs. Before our government there were numerous curriculums that were going on; there were curriculums which preached the king for the kings, and there were curriculums which preached for the communists, and there were curriculums from all these seven parties [the previously mentioned]. So, the Students were confused as to what to study, and the first we have done today is to unify that curriculum, and that's going on.

But we are criticized, and we say that instead of criticism, if you just help us once, that will make a difference. Because criticism will not make a difference. If you [talk?] criticism from New York, thousands of miles away, we don't care. But if you come there and help us, we do care. So actually there are more girls students studying in the faculty of medical sciences than boys are. This is not me who is saying this; it is the United Nations who has announced this. Recently we reopened the faculty of medical science in all major cities of Afghanistan, and in Kandahar there are more girl students than boys! But they are segregated. And the Swedish committees have also established schools for girls. I know they are not enough, but that's what we can do.

So, that is what I say that we have restored. I don't say we are 100% perfect, and nobody will say that they are 100% perfect. We do have shortcomings, and we do need to amend our policies. But we can't do everything over night.

Terrorism

And . . . [another] problem that we are accused of is Terrorism, or the existence of terrorists in Afghanistan. And for Americans terrorism or terrorist means only [Osama] bin Laden. Now . . . bin Laden was in Afghanistan 17 years before even we existed. Bin Laden was in Afghanistan, fought the Soviet Union, and Mr. Ronald Reagan, the president of America in that time, and Mr. Dick Cheney called such people freedom fighters or the heroes of independence because they were fighting for their cause. So Osama bin Laden was one of those guys who was instigated by such media reports, so in that provocation by these countries to go to Afghanistan and fight the Soviets there.

And now when the Soviet Union is fragmented, such people were not needed anymore, and they were transformed into terrorists from heroes to terrorists. So exactly like Mr. Yassir Arafat [Palestinian political leader] was transformed from a terrorist to a hero. So we don't know as to what is the definition of terrorism. We do regret that the terrorists . . . committed actually horrific acts and they were terrorist acts. But if they are terrorist acts, what is the difference between those terrorist acts and the 1998 cruise missile attacks on Afghanistan.

Neither of the two were declared and both of them killed civilians. So we are confused as to what is the definition of terrorism. If it means killing civilians blindly, both of them killed civilians blindly. And the fact is, I'm not going to be offensive or rude; I'm going to be frank. And I think it's sometimes honest to be rude.

If the United States [says] that it has acted for its defense, let's see. The United States government tried to kill a man without even giving him a fair trial. In 1998, they just sent cruise missiles into Afghanistan [in response to the bombing of the U.S. embassy in Kenya] and they announced that they were trying to kill Osama bin Laden. We didn't know Osama bin Laden then. I didn't know him; he was just a simple man. So we were all shocked. I was one of those men who was sitting at home at night. I was called for an immediate council meeting and we all were told the United States have attacked Afghanistan with 75 cruise missiles and trying to kill one man. And they missed that man; killed 19 other students and never apologized for those killings.

So what would you do if you were in our position? If we were to go and send 75 cruise missiles into the United States and say that we were going to kill a man, and we missed that man, and we killed 19 other Americans, what would the United States do? An instant declaration of war. But we were polite. We didn't declare war. We had a lot of problems at home; we didn't want further problem[s].

The Taliban's Diplomatic Efforts Were Rejected

And since then, we are very open-minded on this issue. We have said that if really this man is involved in the Kenya/ Tanzania acts [embassy bombings of 1998], if anybody can give us proof or evidence about his involvement in these horrific acts, we will punish him. Nobody gave us evidence. We put him on trial for 45 days and nobody gave us any kind of evidence.

The fact is that the United States told us they did not believe in our judicial system. We were surprised as to what kind of judicial system they have?! They showed us as to what they are doing to the people. They just tried to kill a man without even giving him a fair trial, even if one of us is a criminal here; the police is not going to blow his house, he must go to a court first. So, that was rejected.

Our first proposal, despite all these things, was rejected. They said they will not believe in our judicial system, and we must give him to New York.

The second proposal that we gave was, we are ready to accept an international monitoring group to come into Afghanistan and monitor this man's activities in Afghanistan. So that he does nothing. Even that he has no telecommunications. That proposal was also rejected. And the third proposal we gave . . . was that we were ready to try or accept a third Islamic country's decision, or the trial in a third Islamic country, with consent of Saudi Arabia and Afghanistan. That was also rejected.

So we don't know, as to what is the problem. If bin Laden was the only issue, we are still very open-minded, and for the fourth time, I'm here, with a letter from my leadership that I'm going to submit to the state department hoping that they will resolve the problem. But I don't think [that] they'll solve the problem. Because we think, and I personally think how that maybe the United States is looking for a Boogy Man always. Remember what [former president of the USSR Mikhail] Gorbachev said? He said, that he's going to do the worst thing ever to the United States. And everybody thought that he's going to blow the United States with nuclear weapon[s]. But he said, I'm going to remove their enemy. And then he fragmented Soviet Union. And he was right. After he fragmented [the] Soviet Union, a lot of people lost their jobs in the Pentagon, in the CIA, and the FBI, because they were not needed anymore.

So we think that maybe these guys are looking for a Boogy Man now. Maybe they want to justify their annual budget; maybe they want to make their citizens feel that they are still needed to defend them. Afghanistan is not a terrorist state; we cannot even make a needle. How are we going to be a terrorist state? How are we going to be a threat to the world?

If the word terrorism is really derived from the word terror, then there are countries making weapons of mass destruction, countries making nuclear weapons, forest deforestation, soil, air, and water pollution. They are terrorist states; we are not. We cannot even make a needle; how are we going to be a threat to the world? So as I said in the beginning, the situation in Afghanistan is not our creation. The situation in Afghanistan reflects the world's image. If you don't like the image in the mirror, do not break the mirror; break your face.

4

The Taliban Demonizes Women Teachers

Hala, as told to Batya Swift Yasgur

This first-person account, told by a former educator and recorded by award-winning freelance writer Batya Swift Yasgur, illustrates how difficult it was for Afghan women to follow both their conscience and their fears for their own safety under the watch of the Taliban religious police. Not officially trained as a teacher, Hala began educating a few little girls in her home after the Taliban outlawed education for women. The narrative describes how her initial modest efforts to tutor a few students grew to a small and eventually coed school that she operated covertly out of her home. Hala's story of being discovered by the Taliban, her beating, the threats on her life, and her flight to another country mirror that of many other Afghan women. She is one of the fortunate few able to tell her story to the outside world.

M y school did not start out as a way of defying the Taliban. It did not even start out as a school. To keep myself alert and stimulated, I went back to my old hobby and pastime—tutoring children. Nadima, my next-door-neighbor and her husband, Zahir, had two daughters named Zakia and Shula, aged ten and seven. Our houses were close by. Surya [her friend and future fellow teacher] and I risked moving between the houses without a male escort.

It started as a conversation with Nadima.

"Zakia is so smart. She was such a good student. Zaki, show Hala your last test."

Zakia ran and brought a math test with an excellent grade. She smiled proudly, then her face clouded over.

"She has been so sad since she has not been allowed to go to school. She is afraid she will forget all she knows. She tries to study the books on her own, but they're too hard for her."

"Would you like me to tutor her?" . . .

Everyone was home-schooling children at that point, so it did not occur to me that I was violating the Taliban's rules. All I felt was excitement. Why hadn't I thought of this before? It was such a pleasure working with ideas, teaching concepts to young children and watching their minds grow.

Zakia and Shula proved to be very cooperative students. Each day they came over and we worked on math, biology, language, and history. They were bright, motivated, and charming. They always asked me for more lessons.

Two weeks later, there was a knock at my door. I opened it to see a woman clad in a a burqa. She was together with her husband. When she came indoors and I could see her face, I recognized her, though I did not know her name. We had seen each other around town, and I had a sort of nodding aquaintanceship with her.

Over tea and cookies, she told me why they had come.

"My daughter Efat says you've been tutoring Zakia and Shula." I nodded.

"Zakia loves going to study with you. She's told Efat all about it. Now Efat wants to come too. Can you work with her?"

Of course I said yes. And yes again to the next mother who asked, and the next. And the next.

"I'm going to need some help with this," I told Surya at the end of the second week. "I already have fifteen children, and more seem to be coming every day. The children are different ages. While I'm working with one student, the others sit and don't do anything. When you have that many kids, it stops being tutoring and you have to run it like a school."

Teaching Is Dangerous

Surya frowned. "Tutoring is one thing. A school is something else. We could get into terrible trouble for running a school. We could be beaten. We could be killed."

"I don't think they'll find out," I said. "None of the parents will tell. It wouldn't make any sense. They would be in as much trouble for sending the children here as we would be for teaching them. And the kids won't tell. So what are we afraid of?"

Surya looked uneasy. "I'll help out," she said finally. "But we'll have to figure out a way to keep this even more secret. I mean, what if someone sees all these kids coming to our house? What are we going to say—that we gave birth to all of them? Without husbands? We could get killed for that too, you know." She laughed, but it was a sad, mirthless sound.

We consulted Haseena [a fellow teacher] and she came up with an idea. "Let's tell them to come separately. No more than two or three at a time. And we'll have two separate shifts. One group will come in the morning at nine. The second group will come at lunchtime, after the others have gone home. We can start class at twelve-thirty.". . .

The Children Are Eager to Learn

Our school grew very quickly. By the end of four months, we had sixty students—thirty in the morning session, thirty in the afternoon. Most of them were girls, but we actually had three boys as well. Many boys' schools had been destroyed in the fighting, including several in our area. I saw no reason why I shouldn't further the education of the boys too. . . .

Some Americans have asked me if I ever had discipline problems with the children. I can honestly say that I didn't. They were well behaved and polite. They knew that they were taking a great risk by coming to our school, but they came anyway, and they were quite eager to learn. If anything, they were insatiable. They were always clamoring for more than we could deliver. "More studies! More lessons!"

We never talked about the danger. If the children had any fears or worries, they either did not express them, or they spoke to their parents. We did not deal with these issues with them. We felt that they were in school to learn, not to discuss problems that we couldn't solve anyway. We also didn't want to scare them. Dwelling on the danger we were in would have undermined their studies and frightened them. So we just went about our business of teaching math, biology, and the other subjects.

The Teachers Weigh the Odds

Of course, we talked among ourselves.

"I don't like it," Surya said one day. "Thirty children at one time. No matter how careful they are, someone is bound to notice them one of these days. There are Religious Police everywhere."

"They don't usually come into our neighborhood," I pointed out. "Not unless someone tips them off."

"But there are so many kids coming and going—" Surya began.

I interrupted. "I'm scared too, but what can we do?"

"We can close the school down." Haseena's voice carried no conviction.

I looked at both of them. "Is that what you want to do?"

Slowly Surya shook her head. "No. I can't bear to do it to the children. They love to come here."

"And what we're doing is important," I said. "I can't see giving up now."

We were having these discussions more and more frequently, as the Taliban reached new heights of brutality. I heard of a woman who was beaten because the Religious Police thought she was walking alone. "She is with me," said a man next to her. "I am her husband." They were both beaten—the husband for allowing his wife to walk in front of him, and the wife for walking in from of her husband. . . .

Despite the fear, those months of running the school were among the happiest I ever had. I felt productive. I felt useful. I felt I was doing something important, something that went beyond myself. I woke up in the morning grateful for the children. I realized that not only was I giving them something, but they were giving me something equally important. Maybe more important. They were giving me something to do with my time and my mind. Each time a child smiled, it lit up my world. The children reminded me that there could be innocence and wonder, even at the darkest times. They gave back to me something basic that I had lost, and I will always be grateful to them for that. . . .

The First Warning

It happened almost five months after we opened the school. An ordinary morning, or so it seemed—that is, if anything after the arrival of the Taliban could be considered "normal." The first shift of students were in the classroom. I was teaching biology. I had gone into the yard to get a leaf to show the children how the veins bring water to a plant.

I didn't hear the knock on the door at first. When it got louder, I thought it was at my neighbor's house. Only when

I heard someone banging hard and shouting did I put on my burqa and answer the door. When I saw who was standing there, I nearly fainted. My knees turned to water. My stomach leaped into my throat and I wanted to throw up. There was no mistaking the white uniform, beard, turban, gun, and unyielding facial expression. I was staring at three members of the Religious Police.

The tallest man scowled at me. "Are you the teacher?"

"Teacher? I don't know what you are talking about."

In my mind, I spoke to the children. I pleaded with them. Please, please stay quiet. Don't move. Don't laugh. And then to God, but without words. A silent prayer for my life. Please.

"I heard there was a school here." The same man was talking.

"You heard the wrong information," I said. "There has been some mistake."

"Tutoring is one thing. A school is something else. We could get into terrible trouble for running a school. We could be beaten. We could be killed."

"Are you sure?" The man tried to peer into the house behind me, but I deliberately stood in the door, blocking his view.

"Really." Could he tell from my voice that I was lying? Well, here was one advantage of the burqa. They could not see my face. I had never thought the burqa could protect me.

He stared at me long and hard. I waited for him to say something. I waited for a child to make some noise that would give us all away. Those moments of waiting seemed to last forever.

"I hope you are telling the truth," he finally said. "Because if you're not, we will punish you severely."

The second man spoke up. "We will come back and kill you."

The first man motioned to the others and they left.

My knees were shaking so badly, I could scarcely walk down the hall. My stomach was still heaving and turning over. My palms were sweating.

Surya saw my face. Right away she knew what had happened.

"Don't say anything to the children," I whispered to her. "I don't want to scare them."

She threw me a frightened look. Then she nodded and returned to class. "So we were up to fractions," I heard her say to the children.

I took a deep breath. I must be brave and strong. Must not let the children see how shaken I am. Must not scare them. Brave and strong. Courage.

When I had calmed down, I entered the class. "Here is the leaf I was going to show you."

Continuing Despite Risk

"Do you want to continue doing this?"

It was night. All the children had gone home. Surya, Haseena, and I were sitting at the table.

"I think so." Surya's voice was so soft, it was almost a whisper. "Every time I think of closing this down, I see the children's faces. I can't bring myself to do it to them."

"That's how I feel," I said.

"I do too, but what if they come back? What if they make good on their threats? They threatened to kill you for this."

"I don't think they will. I think they believed me that there is no school here."

Haseena looked doubtful. "I don't know—"

"They looked like they believed me. They must have done, because they went away without searching the house."

"Maybe we should have a plan, just in case they come again," Surya suggested.

"What kind of plan."

"Where the children can hide if the house is searched."

We talked late into the night, but by morning, we still had not come up with a plan. I yawned. "Let's pick this up again after school."

"What if they come back today?" Haseena asked.

I stood up and walked over to the sink to wash my face. "I don't think they will."

The Taliban Take Their Revenge

I was sitting in the front room of the second floor. We called that room the "office" because that was where we handed out assignments to the children. I looked out the window onto the courtyard, and there they were. Four of them this time. All with guns.

Today they didn't knock. They pushed against the door and stormed through the house. Two of them grabbed my hair and pulled me down the stairs and into the courtyard.

"You lied to us!" It was yesterday's man speaking.

"What are you talking about?" I barely recognized my own voice.

He pulled my hair harder and the other man slapped me. "We know who you are. You come from a family of infidels. Your sister was a Communist. Now she's a Christian. You're a Christian too. Lying and heresy run in your blood." The other man slapped me again, shouting about Christianity and teaching English, a language of the corrupt West.

I do not remember all the rest. I remember the pain. I remember the blows. I remember the feeling of fists against my check. Of hair being wrenched from my scalp. The sound of a woman crying. The sound of children shrieking. The sound of the men shouting. "Children, go home. If we ever catch any one of you in this house again, we will burn down the house with you in it."

The next thing I knew, I was being pulled to my feet by my hair. "You deserve to die," one of the men said.

"And we will come back for you," the other added. "We will make an example of you. Everyone who finds out what you have done and how you have been punished will learn not to sin against God."

He pushed me and I fell. "We'll be back for you tomorrow!" he called, waving, his gun at me.

Assessing the Options

Surya and Haseena came rushing out. They were crying. They hugged me and helped me to my feet. "Are you all right?" Surya kept asking.

I allowed them to support me as I stumbled into the house.

"Are you okay?" I asked them after they had washed my face and bandaged my head. "Did they hurt you?"

Surya shook her head. "They were really after you. Somehow they knew that you've been the main person running this school, that Haseena and I have only been helping out."

"Are the children okay?"

Surya nodded. "They all went home. They were upset and scared, but they weren't hurt."

My head was throbbing and my face was swollen. Clumps of hair were missing, and my scalp was bleeding. Surya brought me an ice pack.

"How do you think they found out about us?" Haseena asked.

"A neighbor—" Surya began.

"No." I remembered what they had said about the family and related it quickly to Surya and Haseena. "They knew specifies about our family."

Surya's eyes widened. "Do you think—"

I nodded. "There's only one way they could have known all this." We did not have to say it aloud. Our own relatives had probably betrayed us. . . . Many of them also belonged to the Religious Police. The Taliban who came to close down my school knew too much about our family. They even knew that Sulima had visited churches during her time in Europe—that's why they assumed that she had converted to Christianity and that I was Christian too. They could not have heard all that information from a stranger. And Taliban did not routinely patrol small residential areas such as ours. They usually came only if someone had reported a violation to them.

"We have to leave here," I said.

Surya nodded. "But where will we go?"

"I will go back to my mother's house," Haseena said. "You can both come too."

"No, that wouldn't work." My headache was getting worse. The ice didn't seem to be helping. "They would think of looking there. We can't stay with family."

"So where will you go?"

I racked my brain to think of someone, anyone, who could hide us. . . .

Surya brought me more ice. "Good idea.". . .

Going into Hiding

"You must come and stay with my family until we come up with another plan," Jabar [a friend who had agreed to help Hala escape] said. He escorted us back home, and we threw some overnight supplies into a suitcase. It did not occur to me to pack identity documents. All I could think of were basics, such as a toothbrush and extra shirts and getting out of the house as fast as possible. I shut the suitcase, then hurried outside. We stood on the doorstep, clinging to one another and crying.

I stepped back and looked at the house that had helped me teach so many wonderful children. Their faces swam before my eyes. Ali, Layli, Zakia, Shula, Efat, I had come to love them, and now I felt as though I was abandoning them. I did not even have the chance to say good-bye.

I didn't have the luxury to reflect for very long. We were in danger every minute we remained. They could come back at any time and make good on their promise to punish me further. We had to leave.

More hugs, kisses, and tears. Then Jabar escorted Haseena to her mother's house. Surya and I followed Jabar to his house.

"You can't stay here very long," Jabar said. "They will probably search the neighborhood houses, looking for you. I live too close by. But I've called my sister. She lives in Now Abad. She said you can stay with her until we can figure out a way to get you out of the country."

As I watched my country get smaller and smaller, I silently prayed for Madarjan, Surya, and all my family.

Out of the country! What about Madarjan? My brothers and sisters? My friends? How could I leave Haseena, Adela, and all my other friends behind? I started to cry.

Jabar's wife came into the room with a handkerchief and a cup of tea. I dried my tears. "You're right," I said to Jabar. "I won't be safe anywhere in the country. I have to leave."

My head was aching where they had pulled my hair and hit me. Dry blood had crusted on my scalp. My back and legs were swollen and painful where they had dragged me and where I fell when they pushed me. Suddenly, I had no more tears. No more feelings. I was numb. Like a robot, I went through the motions. Drinking tea. Lying down and resting. Smiling at Jabar's children. But a part of me had gone elsewhere. My real self was in hiding.

Surya's presence was comforting, even though she couldn't take the pain away. Jabar's wife was also very nice.

So was his sister, whom he took us to after nightfall. "Stay here until I have made arrangements for you," said Jabar. "I know you don't want to leave the country. If I can find a way to get you to the East, where your mother is, I will. Otherwise, I'll arrange for you to go to Pakistan.". . .

"You are going to be my sister," Khaled [Jabar's friend who had arranged for Hala to go the United States] told me as we rode the bus to the border [of Pakistan and Afghanistan]. I nodded.

"What if they for documents? I left mine behind because—"

"It is better that you have no documents because we do not want them to know who you are," Khaled interrupted. "Documents could only get you in trouble. If I handle this correctly, they will believe that I am your brother and we are visiting relatives in Pakistan."

And if they would not believe him? I was too scared to think what might happen then. My heart was thudding. For the first time in my life, I had no family members to talk to or count on. As dangerous as things had been to this point, I always had someone around—my brothers and sisters, Madarjan, my cousins and aunts—to share the dangers. We supported one another. They gave me advice and comfort. Khaled was certainly courteous and gentlemanly, but he was not family. I felt bereft and frightened.

I watched my home country disappear into the distance. Would I ever see it again? Would I ever see Madarjan, Surya, Haseena, Adela, all my family and beloved friends again? They did not even know I was leaving, and it was too dangerous to try to get a message to them. What if I got caught on the border now? They might kill me, or capture and rape me. And what if I got caught on the airplane without a real passport? What did they do to people who traveled with no documents? And what would America be like? Would I be happy in a new, strange country?

At the same time, I felt a sense of excitement and hope. I would be free! No more burqa. No more hiding or lying or secrecy. I could walk anywhere or do anything. If I made it to the United States, my problems would be over. . . .

Leaving Afghanistan Behind

As Khaled had predicted, the man [a man with documents to get Hala into the United States] had no difficulty getting me onto a plane. We walked like any other good Muslim couple, with me a few paces behind him, through the hallways of the airport. I didn't know what airline I was flying. I didn't know what name I was supposed to be using. Nothing. I just followed the man blindly. Like an obedient Muslim woman.

He handed the documents to the official. I don't know what they said to each other. It was common enough for men to handle all transactions for their wives so that the wife wouldn't have communication with a male other than her husband, so this didn't strike the official as unusual. Besides, it was clear that the man had done this before. The official knew him. Few words were exchanged, and the official pointed to a door. I walked through an enclosed corridor onto the plane.

As I watched my country get smaller and smaller, I silently prayed for Madarjan, Surya, and all my family.

And for the country itself.

Chapter 3

The U.S. War and the Fall of the Taliban

1

The United States Should Attack Afghanistan to Overthrow the Taliban

Charles Krauthammer

Following the September 11, 2001, terrorist attacks on America, the U.S. government quickly determined that the terrorist group al Qaeda (the base) was responsible for the attacks. At the time, al Qaeda's leader, Osama bin Laden, was living in Afghanistan under the protection of the Taliban government. U.S. officials demanded that the Taliban turn over bin Laden to America. The Taliban refused to cooperate with this demand, and the U.S. government launched a military campaign against the Taliban on October 7, 2001. Within weeks the Taliban had been driven from power by forces of the United States and the Northern Alliance, the group of Afghanis opposed to the Taliban.

Prior to the U.S. attack, many in the West debated whether such a war was necessary or justified. In the following selection, written prior to the U.S. invasion, syndicated columnist Charles Krauthammer argues that attacking Afghanistan to destroy the Taliban is a necessary first step in America's war against terrorism. The Taliban shares responsibility for the attacks on America, he contends, and must be punished accordingly.

Charles Krauthammer, "Dear Nations: Harbor Terrorists, and Your Regime Dies," *The Record*, September 28, 2001, p. L7. Copyright © 2001 by The Washington Post Writers Group. Reproduced by permission.

Yes, we need to get Osama bin Laden. Yes, we need to bring down the terrorist networks. But the overriding aim of the war on terrorism is changing regimes. And it starts with the Taliban.

Searching Afghan caves for Bin Laden is precisely the trap he would wish us to fall into. Terrorists cannot operate without the succor and protection of governments. The planet is divided into countries. Unless terrorists want to camp in Antarctica, they must live in sovereign states. The objective of this war must be to make it impossible or intolerable for any state to harbor, protect, or aid and abet terrorists. The point is not to swat every mosquito, but to drain the swamp.

The Taliban share responsibility for the worst mass murder in American history.

The war begins in Afghanistan. The first objective must be to destroy the Taliban regime. Indeed, to make an example of the Taliban, to show the world—and especially regimes engaged in terrorism—that President [George W.] Bush was serious when he told the nation that we make no distinction between the terrorists and the governments that harbor them. The take-home lesson must be: Harbor terrorists—and your regime dies.

Remember the context. Radical Islam is riding a wave of victories: The bombing of the Marine barracks in 1983 that drove the United States out of Lebanon, the killing of 18 American soldiers in Mogadishu in 1993 that drove the United States out of Somalia, and, in between, the war that drove the other superpower, the Soviet Union, out of Afghanistan.

And now Sept. 11, which sent America into shock and leaves it deep in fear. Victory breeds victory. The terrorists feel invincible, and those sitting on the fence in the region are waiting to see whether they really are. Overthrowing the Taliban would reverse the historical tide and profoundly affect the psychological balance of power.

America Must Not Lose Its Nerve

This step is so obvious and necessary that it is deeply troubling to see the secretary of state [Colin Powell] begin to wobble. If the Taliban give up Bin Laden and al Qaeda (his terrorist network), said Powell on [Sept. 25, 2001], "we wouldn't be worrying about whether they are the regime in power or not." He then offered carrots ("significant benefits . . . a better relationship with the West") and even hinted at American aid.

Carrots? Aid? After Sept. 11? The Taliban share responsibility for the worst mass murder in American history. For that they must be made to pay, or what meaning is there to the president's pledge that "justice will be done"? If the administration goes wobbly on the Taliban, it might as well give up the war on terrorism before it starts. The Taliban are dripping blood. They are totally isolated. They are militarily vulnerable. On the ground they face a fierce armed opposition, the Northern Alliance, that is ready and eager to take Kabul. With our support, it could.

It may not be easy and it may not be quick. But such a signal victory is essential.

The campaign, however, cannot stop there. Nor with Bin Laden. (Although when the Taliban government falls, finding Bin Laden and his associates will be that much easier.) Afghanistan is just stage one.

The Taliban Are Only Part of the Problem

A logical stage two is Syria. It harbors a myriad of terrorist groups, but the regime is as rational as it is cynical. Syria has no ideological or religious affinity with the terrorists it supports. It uses them to advance geopolitical aims. It can therefore be persuaded to abandon them.

We know this. For years, Damascus harbored Abdullah Ocalan, the leader of the PKK (Kurdish Workers' Party), which was fighting the government in Turkey. Turkey repeatedly demanded that Syria turn him over. Syria refused. Until October 1998, when Turkey massed troops on its Syrian border, threatening military action. Ocalan was shortly expelled from Damascus. He now sits in a Turkish jail.

Syria is terrorist. But Syria is pliable. It is a low-hanging fruit. After Afghanistan, we turn to Damascus. What then? Stage three is Iraq and Iran, obviously the most difficult and dangerous. Which is why it would be foolish to take them on right away. Changing regimes in Kabul and changing policy in Damascus, however, would already have radically changed the regional dynamic by demonstrating American power in a region where power, above all, commands respect.

In Iran, where the conservative clerics are unpopular and a large Westernized middle class is already straining for a free society, change might come from within. In Iraq, although Saddam is detested, internal revolt is less likely. Saddam will make his stand and we will have to confront the most dangerous terrorist regime in the world. The war on terrorism will conclude in Baghdad. How? No one knows. All we do know is that history, cunning and cruel, will demand that if this president wants victory in the war he has declared, he will have to achieve it on the very spot where his own father [George H.W. Bush], 10 years ago, let victory slip away.

2

The United States Should Not Attack Afghanistan to Overthrow the Taliban

Tamim Ansary

Writer and Afghani immigrant Tamim Ansary questioned the early passionate calls for bombing Afghanistan in retaliation for the September 11, 2001, terrorist attacks. In the following editorial written before the war started, Ansary asserted that bombing Afghanistan would only further harm civilians rather than the intended target—the Taliban. He pleaded with Americans to see that not only were the common Afghani people not members of the Taliban, they themselves had long been terrorized by the Taliban's extremist policies. Ansary argued that only a ground war with potential heavy American casualties offered any chance to destroy the Taliban and Osama bin Laden. He also maintained that such a war was undesirable because it would result in a much broader and lengthier conflict with the Muslim world than Americans were prepared for.

I've been hearing a lot of talk about "bombing Afghanistan back to the Stone Age." Ronn Owens, on San Francisco's KGO Talk Radio, conceded [September 14, 2001] that this would mean killing innocent people, people who had nothing to do with this atrocity [the September 11, 2001, attacks on America], but "we're at war, we have to accept collateral damage. What else can we do?" Minutes later I heard some TV pundit discussing whether we "have the belly to do what must be done."

And I thought about the issues being raised especially hard because I am from Afghanistan, and even though I've lived in the United States for 35 years I've never lost track of what's going on there. So I want to tell anyone who will listen how it all looks from where I'm standing.

I speak as one who hates the Taliban and Osama bin Laden. There is no doubt in my mind that these people were responsible for the atrocity in New York. I agree that something must be done about those monsters.

But the Taliban and bin Laden are not Afghanistan. They're not even the government of Afghanistan. The Taliban are a cult of ignorant psychotics who took over Afghanistan in 1997. Bin Laden is a political criminal with a plan. When you think Taliban, think Nazis. When you think bin Laden, think Hitler. And when you think "the people of Afghanistan" think "the Jews in the concentration camps." It's not only that the Afghan people had nothing to do with this atrocity. They were the first victims of the perpetrators. They would exult if someone would come in there, take out the Taliban and clear out the rats' nest of international thugs holed up in their country.

Afghan Civilians Are the Ultimate Victims

Some say, why don't the Afghans rise up and overthrow the Taliban? The answer is, they're starved, exhausted, hurt, incapacitated, suffering. A few years ago, the United Nations estimated that there are 500,000 disabled orphans in Afghanistan—a country with no economy, no food. There are millions of widows. And the Taliban has been burying these widows alive in mass graves. The soil is littered with land mines, the farms were all destroyed by the Soviets. These are a few of the reasons why the Afghan people have not overthrown the Taliban.

We come now to the question of bombing Afghanistan back to the Stone Age. Trouble is, that's been done. The Soviets took care of it already. Make the Afghans suffer? They're already suffering. Level their houses? Done. Turn their schools into piles of rubble? Done. Eradicate their hospitals? Done. Destroy their infrastructure? Cut them off from medicine and health care? Too late. Someone already did all that. New bombs would only stir the rubble of earlier bombs. Would they at least get the Taliban? Not likely. In today's Afghanistan, only the Taliban eat, only they have the means to move around. They'd slip away and hide. Maybe the bombs would get some of those disabled orphans; they don't move too fast, they don't even have wheelchairs. But flying over Kabul and dropping bombs wouldn't really be a strike against the criminals who did this horrific thing. Actually it would only be making common cause with the Taliban—by raping once again the people they've been raping all this time.

So what else is there? What can be done, then? Let me now speak with true fear and trembling. The only way to get Bin Laden is to go in there with ground troops. When people speak of "having the belly to do what needs to be done" they're thinking in terms of having the belly to kill as many as needed. Having the belly to overcome any moral qualms about killing innocent people. Let's pull our heads out of the sand. What's actually on the table is Americans dying. And not just because some Americans would die fighting their way through Afghanistan to bin Laden's hideout. It's much bigger than that, folks. Because to get any troops to Afghanistan, we'd have to go through Pakistan. Would they let us? Not likely. The conquest of Pakistan would have to be first. Will other Muslim nations just stand by? You see where I'm going. We're flirting with a world war between Islam and the West.

And guess what: That's bin Laden's program. That's exactly what he wants. That's why he did this. Read his speeches and statements. It's all right there. He really believes Islam would beat the West. It might seem ridiculous, but he figures if he can polarize the world into Islam and the West, he's got a billion soldiers. If the West wreaks a holocaust in those lands, that's a billion people with nothing left to lose; that's even better from bin Laden's point of view. He's probably wrong—in the end the West would win, whatever that would mean—but the war would last for years and millions would die, not just theirs but ours.

Who has the belly for that? Bin Laden does. Anyone else?

3

The War Against the Taliban Must Be Uncompromising

John McCain

In the following editorial written during the U.S. war in Afghanistan, Republican senator from Arizona John McCain stressed that America must not hesitate in its resolve to defend itself and the rest of the world from terrorists despite accusations that it was waging war against all Islam rather than Islamic militants. The nation must also proceed quickly and wholeheartedly, he continued, despite a grievous awareness that to destroy the Taliban regime it would be necessary to jeopardize Afghani civilians. Holding back on the amount of ground and air forces needed in Afghanistan would only prolong the suffering of the Afghani civilians, more of whom would survive in the long run if America won a decisive and permanent victory.

War is a miserable business. The lives of a nation's finest patriots are sacrificed. Innocent people suffer and die. Commerce is disrupted, economies are damaged. Strategic interests shielded by years of patient statecraft are endangered as the exigencies of war and diplomacy conflict. However heady the appeal of a call to arms, however just the cause, we should still shed a tear for all that will be lost when war claims its wages from as. Shed a tear, and then get on with the business of killing our enemies as quickly as we can, and as ruthlessly us we must.

There is no avoiding the war we are in today, any more than we could have avoided world war after our fleet was bombed at Pearl Harbor. America is under attack by a depraved, malevolent force that opposes our every interest and hates every value we hold dear. We must expect and prepare for our enemies to strike us again. As in all wars we must endure before we prevail. Only the complete destruction of international terrorism and the regimes that sponsor it will spare America from further attack.

We did not cause this war. Our enemies did, and they are to blame for the deprivations and difficulties it occasions.

As the president has explained, this war will have many components. But American military power is the most important part. When it is brought to bear in great and terrible measure it is a thing to strike terror in the heart of anyone who opposes it. No mountain is big enough, no cave deep enough to hide from the full fury of American power. Yet our enemies harbor doubts that America will use force with a firm determination to achieve our ends, that we will use all force necessary to achieve unconditional victory. We need to persuade them otherwise, immediately.

Fighting this war in half measures will only give our enemies time and opportunity to strike us again. We must change permanently the mindset of terrorists and those parts of Islamic populations who believe the terrorist conceit that they will prevail because America has not the stomach to wage a relentless, long-term, and, at times, ruthless war to destroy them. We cannot fight this war from the air alone. We cannot fight it without casualties. And we cannot fight it without risking unintended damage to humanitarian and political interests.

American Attacks Not Anti-Muslim

The United States is not waging war against a religion or a race. For too long our enemies have been allowed, even by America's purported friends in the region, to sow their hatred of us throughout the Islamic world. Should the conduct of our war incidentally help inflame that hatred it may indeed increase the threat to regimes in the Middle East and elsewhere whose stability is a strategic interest of the United States. But that threat will be infinitely greater should we fail in our mission or delay victory by one day longer than necessary.

We must reject appeals to suspend military operations to accommodate the religious practices of affected populations. Fighting during Ramadan is no more a war against Islam than fighting during Hanukkah and Christmas is a war against Judaism and Christianity. Nor should we agree to a cease-fire to feed starving Afghans. It wouldn't work anyway. The Taliban have no interest in feeding their people. Their only aim is to prevent our victory, and only our victory will alleviate the suffering of innocent Afghans.

The Taliban Must Be Rooted Out

It is clear that to destroy bin Laden and his associates we will first need to destroy the regime that protects them. To achieve that end, we cannot allow the Taliban safe refuge among the civilian population. We must destroy them, wherever they hide. That will surely increase the terrible danger facing noncombatants, a regrettable but necessary fact of war. But it will also shorten the days they must suffer war's cruel reality.

Nor should we delay or shrink from helping these Afghans committed to the destruction of our enemies. The Northern Alliance wants to destroy the Taliban regime. So do we. That is reason enough to give them all the air support and other assistance they need to take Mazar-e-Sharif, Kabul and any other Taliban territory they can conquer just as quickly as possible.

We have been sparing in the amount of ordinance we have dropped on the Taliban front lines. We have not yet employed B-2s and B-52s, the most destructive weapons in our airborne arsenal, against them. We shouldn't fight this war in increments. The Taliban and their terrorist allies are indeed tough fighters. They'll need to experience a more impressive display of American firepower before they contemplate surrender.

Munitions dumps and air defenses are necessary targets. But so are the Taliban soldiers. Those soldiers and their commanders will not become dispirited, abandon the regime, and become intelligence assets in our war against terrorists until a great many of their comrades have been killed by the United States armed forces.

The president of Pakistan, Gen. Pervez Musharraf, has been our good and steadfast ally in a war that would, if unsuccessful, threaten his regime. Pakistan has a legitimate interest in who rules its chronically unstable eastern neighbor. But al Qaeda and time, not the violence of our campaign, nor the ups and downs of Afghan politics, are the greater threats to our friend's interests and to ours. Keeping our priorities straight will serve all our interests best.

Terrorism Must Be Wiped Out

We have a great many interests in the world that were, until September 11, of the first order of magnitude, and the central occupation of American statesmen. No longer. Now we have only one primary occupation, and that is to vanquish international terrorism. Not reduce it. Not change its operations. Not temporarily subdue it. But vanquish it. It is a difficult and demanding task that will affect many other important interests, favorably in the long run, but in the short run, in some instances, unfavorably. That cannot be helped, and we should not make victory on the battlefield more difficult to achieve so that our diplomacy is easier to conduct.

We did not cause this war. Our enemies did, and they are to blame for the deprivations and difficulties it occasions. They are to blame for the loss of innocent life. They are to blame for the geopolitical problems confronting our friends and us. We can help repair the damage of war. But to do so, we must destroy the people who started it.

Veterans of war live forever with the memory of war's merciless nature, of the awful things that had to be done by their hand. They did not recoil from their terrible duty because they knew that the freedom they defended was worth dying and killing for.

War is a miserable business. Let's get on with it.

4

A Victim's Family Member Opposes the War in Afghanistan

Rita Lasar

Rita Lasar, whose brother died in the September 11, 2001, attack on the World Trade Center, is an outspoken critic of America's war on Afghanistan. Since she and other relatives of victims visited Afghanistan, she has tried to tell as many people as possible that the Afghani people are innocent victims of terrorists both outside their country and within it.

I ran into a neighbor's apartment—she faces what was the World Trade Center—and was in time to see the second plane hit. I said to myself, 'Oh my God, my brother Abey—my baby brother—works in that building.' I called my other brother, Jackie. He and my sister-in-law had been on the phone with Abey when they heard about the plane hitting, screaming at him to get out. He said, 'I can't leave Ed'—his office mate, a very dear friend, a quadriplegic in a wheelchair. He said, 'Ed can't leave and I'm not going to leave him. I'm going to wait till help comes.'

And help came too late.

On the following Friday, President [George W.] Bush gave a speech at a memorial in the National Cathedral and he mentioned my brother's act. I realized that my country was going to use my brother's act as justification for going to war in Afghanistan. I absolutely disagreed with it.

Rita Lasar, "In Their Own Words: Rita Lasar," www.thejewishweek.com, September 5, 2002. Copyright © 2002 by Rita Lasar. Reproduced by permission.

The drums of war started beating and I was asked to speak at peace rallies. A woman who I had never heard of, from a group in San Francisco, Global Exchange, called me and said, 'Rita, would you like to go to Afghanistan?'

I said yes.

We gathered a small group of people who had lost relatives on Sept. 11 and went to Afghanistan for two weeks. I hoped that by meeting people who like me had lost people through this act of violence that somehow we could connect with each other and grieve with each other.

I encountered war—not the television images—for the first time in my life. We brought gifts, we brought money. We met orphans, we met widows, we met widowers, we met street children, we met farmers who could no longer go back to their farms because cluster bombs surrounded their land.

Everybody in Afghanistan knew about Sept. 11. They thought we would hate them, that we would have nothing to do with them.

Everybody in Afghanistan knew about Sept. 11. They thought we would hate them, that we would have nothing to do with them. They did not know there were Americans who did not blame the ordinary people.

The grace and the kindness and the goodness of the people I met overwhelmed me. All the people we met expressed such sorrow for what had happened to us that I was shamed by their goodness.

After we came back we formed a group called Peaceful Tomorrows, under which we speak about alternatives to violence. I'm going to Hiroshima [city bombed by the United States during World War II] and I'm going to other places in Japan to talk about the same thing.

5

The Taliban Has Regained Strength

Ilana Ozernoy

Although U.S.-led forces drove the Taliban from power in October 2001, they did not completely eliminate the movement. In the following selection, Ilana Ozernoy, a reporter for *U.S. News & World Report*, explains that the Taliban has regrouped since the end of major fighting. Thought by many to have been debilitated by allied troops, the resilient Taliban is cobbling together troops and ammunition and waging guerrilla attacks. Unable to see evidence that their lives will improve under Hamid Karzai's U.S.-backed transitional government, many people throughout Afghanistan are looking once again to the Taliban for stability and leadership.

A s the sun drops behind a curtain of mountains in eastern Afghanistan, a golden dust rises above this busy border crossing [Spin Boldak, Afghanistan]. On foot, donkey cart, rickshaw, and jangling Pakistani truck, a steady stream of anonymous faces spills past a symbolic green fence, unhindered by even a cursory check. They are merchants and refugees, travelers and, perhaps, Taliban fighters. Mohammed Ismael, his eyes focused on the small hammer he uses to mend ersatz Adidas sneakers and black, faux-leather shoes, figures that thousands of people pass through daily—though, he shrugs, "no one can tell you the exact number."

The bustle of this border town is a sign of normalcy—

Ilana Ozernoy, "Afghanistan: The Return of the Taliban," *U.S. News & World Report*, September 29, 2003. Copyright © 2003 by U.S. News & World Report, L.P. All rights reserved. Reproduced with permission.

and a cause for alarm. Afghanistan's war-scarred eastern and southern provinces are under a fresh spate of attacks by pro-Taliban guerrillas, some crossing into Afghanistan after being sheltered and stirred to action at Pakistan's fundamentalist madrasahs [religious schools]. . . . American troops from the U.S. Army's 10th Mountain Division and their Afghan allies in Operation Mountain Viper have been going after as many as 1,000 Taliban and foreign fighters hiding out in the mountainous region northeast of here.

The Talibs may not be able to directly take on the 11,500 U.S. and coalition troops tasked with hunting members of the old regime and al Qaeda, but they know how to play an insurgent's game. Groups of five to 10 fighters stage small-scale attacks—executions of aid workers, assassinations of moderate mullahs and government officials, and hand grenades and jury-rigged explosives directed against coalition forces. At night, the Taliban wages a public relations campaign, dropping "night letters" at mosques, calling on locals to join the resistance.

U.S. Military Downplays Resurgence

U.S. Army Col. Burke Garrett, commander of Coalition Task Force Warrior, downplays the impact of the "neo-Taliban." The enemy, he says, includes foreign fighters on "jihadi tours" who tote camcorders to record their exploits. "They videotape themselves so they can go back to Pakistan and get paid," he says.

If they survive. One video, recently plucked from a dead fighter, shows a guerrilla launching a rocket, followed by the scene of a man in Afghan garb rigging an explosive device. The image hits home for Garrett: "That's the mine that killed one of my soldiers." Two American soldiers were killed in recent fighting, bringing the two-year total to 30 American military deaths from hostile fire, though the toll has been far greater among allied Afghans. Some 200 Taliban fighters reportedly have been killed in . . . three weeks [in September 2003] in the most intense fighting in more than a year. . . .

As in Iraq, U.S. forces are facing a combination of foreign fighters and homegrown resistance. In the conservative south, where much of the opposition is concentrated, a Talib can find shelter in any kebab house [restaurant serving kebabs]. "The Taliban were always in Afghanistan," says

Khalid Pushtun of President Hamid Karzai's Kandahar office. "They stayed in their houses, in their villages. They were just waiting for some kind of green light to start fighting the American and Afghan authorities."

That green light is a rising anger among some Afghans at what they regard as America's unfulfilled promise of reconstruction. Outside of Kabul, powerful warlords reign, and international aid has been slow to make a difference in daily life. For [2004], the Bush administration is budgeting $12.2 billion for Afghanistan: $11 billion for U.S. military costs and $1.2 billion for reconstruction, including $564 million for border guards, police, and the Afghan Army.

Taliban Takes Advantage of Slow Reconstruction

The volatile southeastern provinces, the old Taliban heartland, are sliding into a self-reinforcing cycle of instability: Because of attacks on aid workers, international aid organizations have all but pulled out, and curtailed aid work has discouraged international donors, further slowing reconstruction. "The Taliban want to show Afghans, 'Look at these foreigners . . . they are all liars,'" says a man calling himself Mullah Ismael, who allies himself with the Taliban. Tall, reed-thin, with piercing blue eyes and leathery skin, he met clandestinely with *U.S. News* in a desolate village of Helmand province, three hours southwest of Kandahar. "The [current Afghan] government and the West is like an elephant, and we are like mosquitoes," he says. "We want the enemy to become weaker and weaker, to get malaria and die from the disease."

"The Taliban want to show Afghans, 'Look at these foreigners . . . they are all liars.'"

Ismael, who says he held an important security position in the former Taliban government, describes a strategy of guerrilla warfare to destabilize [Afghani transitional leader Hamid] Karzai's government and force the Americans out. He tells of weapons depots hidden in the hillsides, furtive instructions delivered by anonymous Taliban underlings, and attacks on "NGO spies," by which he means Afghans working for foreign nongovernmental organizations doing aid work. "The current government doesn't let us conduct religious studies," Ismael complains, explaining the lure of Pakistani madrasahs. "I am ready to sacrifice peace and stability for Islam.". . .

In this part of the country, the Taliban doesn't have to fight hard to convince a discontented population. In the village of Girishk, two hours from Kandahar, an old man named Shir Ali tacitly divulges ties to the Taliban. "Everywhere there is insecurity and there is no reconstruction," he asserts. "That's why people support us." Shir Ali says he has attended underground Taliban shuras, or meetings, which take place in the folds of the mountains that hug the village. "The Taliban recruit by reminding people of the time when there was no murder, there were no attacks, and there was a real presence of Islam," he says.

The Taliban Blend and Hide Easily

And the Taliban can move about without attracting unwanted attention. They look like "any other Afghan," says U.S. Army Capt. Toby Moore, who led several missions against insurgents in Zabul province, east of Kandahar. He says the fighters carry small arms they can easily ditch to blend into a crowd, which makes them difficult to identify.

To western eyes, that may be true. But Afghans can read the subtle signs delineating friend from foe. In the madrasahs, the Taliban are taught to speak in calm, controlled tones, and they often pepper their speech with Arabic. The way a man wears his turban can mark him as a Talib and even show where he's from; a Talib from Helmand province keeps the bulky intersection of cloth wrapped around his head above one of his ears, but a Talib from Kandahar positions it at the nape of his neck.

The police chief of the southern province of Helmand has no doubts that he is in the minority. Amunallah, a stocky man with an easy laugh, figures 70 percent of Helmand's population supports the Taliban, and he even retains a number of Taliban subordinates to keep the peace. Barreling through Helmand's desert expanse in his Toyota station wagon, with the dust rising behind him like puffs of white smoke, Amunallah is always flanked by a ragged crew of armed guards for protection. But in the Taliban belt, it is U.S. military power that counts most. "We are relying completely on the Americans," says Haji Abdulruf, deputy police chief of Girishk. "If there were no Americans, I'm sure the Taliban would take over in two hours."

Anti-Taliban Afghans say that with America's September 11 tragedy, the interests of the world's most powerful nation and one of its poorest have converged. "Before 9/11, we would cry to the world to save us from these cruel men [the Taliban]. But after 9/11, it was the world that was crying," says Amunallah. The enemy lurks in the darkness, so the commander makes haste to get home. "We got lucky when the U.S. was attacked," he says, clambering into his station wagon as the sunset brings the perils of another night. Border crossings U.S. troops are battling Taliban fighters near Pakistan. In Afghanistan and Iraq, unguarded borders permit easy entry for foreign fighters.

Chronology

329–327 B.C.
Alexander the Great conquers the region that will later become Afghanistan.

7th–18th Centuries
Muslim conquest; various Islamic rulers vie for control.

1747–1818
The Durrani Dynasty unites most of the region.

1826–1863
Emir Dost Mohammad reigns.

1838–1842
The First Afghan War is waged between the British and the Afghans.

1878
The Second Afghan War takes place.

1893
The Durand Agreement establishes the modern-day borders of Afghanistan.

1907
The British guarantee Afghan independence but maintain control of foreign affairs.

1919
The Third Afghan War ends in complete independence for Afghanistan.

1933–1973
King Mohammad Zahir Shah rules the country, first under the guidance of relatives and then, after 1963, on his own.

1964
Afghanistan's first constitution rules that women and men are legally equal. This and other liberal dictates in the document anger rural Afghans and create political problems.

1973
King Zahir Shah is overthrown in a military coup.

1978
The People's Democratic Party of Afghanistan takes over the country in a military coup.

1979
The USSR invades Afghanistan and takes over the government.

1987–1988
The Soviets withdraw from Afghanistan and install Mohammad Najibullah as president.

1987–1992
A civil war between warring mujahideens rages.

1992
President Najibullah's government collapses.

1992–1994
Mujahideen are the official government of Afghanistan.

November 1994
The Taliban captures Kandahar.

September 1995
The Taliban captures Herat. The Taliban bans the education of women.

September 1996
The Taliban captures Jalalabad and Kabul, causing ten thousand people to leave Jalalabad for Pakistan. The USSR takes an official position against the Taliban.

October 1996
The Taliban takes Badghis Province. The United Nations asks all countries to oppose the Taliban because of its poor treatment of women. Fifty thousand people leave Kabul for Pakistan.

1997
May: The Taliban fails in an attempt to takeover Mazar-e Sharif. Two hundred thousand people flee to Kabul after having been evacuated from their homes in northern Afghanistan. The Voice of Sharia, the Taliban-run radio sta-

tion, broadcasts a defense of the Taliban's treatment of the Afghan people.

July: An oil pipeline construction agreement is signed between Pakistan, Turkmenistan, Delta Oil of Saudi Arabia, and UNOCAL of the United States.

August 1998
The Taliban captures Mazar-e Sharif. The United States bombs targets in Afghanistan, believing Osama bin Laden, the leader of the terrorist group al Qaeda, who had official asylum there, was responsible for attacks on U.S. embassies in the Middle East.

1999
The UN Security Council imposes sanctions on the Taliban.

2000
September: The Taliban captures Taliqan in the northeast. About 170,000 people leave Taliqan for Pakistan; 80,000 more are displaced but remain in Afghanistan.

December: The UN Security Council imposes more sanctions on the Taliban.

2001
September 11: Terrorists attack the World Trade Center and the Pentagon. The United States believes Osama bin Laden is behind the attacks.

October 7: After the Taliban refuses to turn Bin Laden over to the United States, the United States begins bombing strategic Taliban sites in Afghanistan. Bin Laden issues a statement calling on all Muslims to wage a holy war against America. Pro-Taliban, anti-U.S. demonstrations erupt in Pakistan.

October 19: The United States begins ground assaults against the Taliban with the aid of Afghan resistance fighters known as the Northern Alliance.

October 26: The Taliban executes former mujahideen leader Abdul Haq, his nephew, and anti-Taliban commander Haji Dawran for treason and espionage.

November 9: The Northern Alliance forces take cities of Mazar-e Sharif and Taliqan from the Taliban.

November 11: Several international journalists are killed in a Taliban ambush.

November 12: The Northern Alliance captures Herat and moves on Kabul.

November 13: The Northern Alliance seizes Kabul. The Taliban retreats from Kandahar.

November 15: The Taliban leaves Kandahar.

November 21: Taliban commanders in Kunduz meet with Northern Alliance leaders to negotiate a surrender. The Taliban claims to still control the provinces of Kandahar, Helmand, Uruzgan, Zabol, and part of Ghazni Province. The Taliban claims not to know the whereabouts of Osama bin Laden.

November 24: The Taliban surrenders Kunduz.

November 25: Hundreds of U.S. Marines land near Kandahar to fight Taliban and al Qaeda on the ground.

November 27: Afghan leaders meet with UN representatives in Bonn, Germany, to work out guidelines for a post-Taliban government.

November 29: The United States continues air strikes on Kandahar. Mullah Omar, the top Taliban leader, urges Taliban forces to keep fighting.

December 5: Hamid Karzai is selected as interim leader of Afghanistan by delegates in Bonn.

December 9: The Taliban surrenders Kandahar and withdraws from the city. Former Taliban soldiers infiltrate nearby villages and continue to enforce Taliban rules.

December 11: Bin Laden and his men retreat to mountains near Tora Bora in eastern Afghanistan. The United States bombs a complex of caves in the hopes of killing Bin Laden.

December 16: The United States declares that al Qaeda has been removed from Afghanistan. The U.S. embassy in Kabul reopens.

December 20: Afghan officials agree to the presence of a UN peacekeeping force in the hopes of rebuilding Afghanistan.

December 22: Hamid Karzai is sworn in as chairman of an interim government. The United States officially recognizes the Afghan government for the first time since 1979.

December 26: U.S. forces continue to hunt for Bin Laden near Tora Bora.

2002

January: The Taliban admits defeat. Seven top Taliban officials who surrendered at Kandahar are released, and it is assumed that they leave the country.

February: The United States continues to bomb Taliban and al Qaeda sites and search for Mullah Omar and Osama bin Laden. Taliban and al Qaeda prisoners of war are imprisoned at the U.S. naval station at Guantánamo Bay in Cuba.

March: The United States begins Operation Anaconda, in which U.S. and Afghan soldiers try to force the remaining Taliban and al Qaeda fighters from the country.

April: Former king Zahir Shah returns but makes no claim on the throne.

May: Allied forces continue their military campaign to route remaining soldiers of al Qaeda and the Taliban from the southeast.

June 11: The *loya jirga*, or grand council, opens.

June 13: The *loya jirga* elects Karzai as interim head of state. Karzai selects members of his administration, which is to serve until 2004.

July: Vice President Haji Abdul Qadir is assassinated by gunmen in Kabul. A U.S. air raid in Uruzgan Province kills forty-eight civilians, many of them members of a wedding party.

September: Hamid Karzai is nearly assassinated by a Taliban assassin.

October: The top UN envoy in Afghanistan tells the UN Security Council that the new Afghan government headed by Karzai does not have the power to deal with the underlying problems that cause security threats in the country.

November: Rival factions in northern Afghanistan begin turning in their weapons as part of a UN program to curb violence. Former king Zahir Shah inaugurates a special committee to draft a new constitution for the country.

December: Afghan commander Amanullah Khan launches an attack on positions held by Ismail Khan, governor of Herat Province.

2003

January: The Afghan security chief claims that minor clashes have been reported between Afghan forces and suspected members of the Taliban. Karzai announces the formation of four commissions to accelerate the disarmament of warlord armies and to rebuild the Afghan National Army.

February: President Karzai visits the U.S. Senate Foreign Relations Committee in Washington, D.C. In the hearing,

Karzai gives an optimistic view of the state of Afghanistan and disputes claims that one hundred thousand militiamen living in the provinces are beyond the control of his government. Factional fighting flares up between rival Afghan groups within seven hundred yards of the perimeter of Bagram Air Base.

March: The first foreign aid worker is killed in Afghanistan since the Taliban was removed from power. There is a surge of attacks against U.S. troops in southern Afghanistan. The United States launches Operation Valiant Strike in Kandahar, the largest U.S. mission in Afghanistan since Operation Anaconda. Afghan authorities raid a house in Kandahar and arrest ten former Taliban members. Police seize arms, explosives, and land mines. The first Afghan radio station programmed solely for women begins broadcasting in Kabul.

April: Officials announce a UN program to disarm, demobilize, and reintegrate an estimated one hundred thousand fighters across Afghanistan in the next three years. Nearly fifty suspected Taliban fighters attack a checkpoint in the Shingai district of Zabul Province; the fighters flee after a brief battle.

May: Defense Secretary Donald Rumsfeld declares that Afghanistan is now secure, despite evidence that pro-Taliban soldiers continue to attack government buildings, U.S. bases, and aid workers on a daily basis. Afghanistan's membership in the International Criminal Court (ICC) takes effect. The ICC will have the authority to investigate and prosecute serious war crimes and crimes against humanity committed on Afghan soil.

June: Clashes in Kandahar between Taliban loyalists and government forces leave forty-nine people dead.

August: NATO assumes charge of security in Kabul.

September: U.S.-led forces fight back a group of Taliban rebels.

December: The U.S. military begins Operation Avalanche, which involves some two thousand soldiers.

2004

January: At the *loya jirga*, leaders adopt a new constitution with provisions for a strong centralized government and presidency.

September: The first free elections are scheduled to take place in Afghanistan.

For Further Research

Books

Sally Armstrong, *Veiled Threat: The Hidden Power of the Women of Afghanistan*. New York: Four Walls Eight Windows, 2002.

Peter Bergen, *Holy War, Inc.: Inside the Secret World of Osama bin Laden*. New York: Free Press, 2001.

Burchard Brentjes and Helga Brentjes, *Taliban: A Shadow over Afghanistan*. Varanasi, India: Rishi, 2000.

Antonio Donini, Norah Niland, and Karin Wermester, eds., *Nation-Building Unraveled?: Aid, Peace, and Justice in Afghanistan*. Bloomfield, CT: Kumarian, 2004.

David Edwards, *Before Taliban: Genealogies of the Afghan Jihad*. Berkeley: University of California Press, 2002.

Deborah Ellis, *The Breadwinner*. Toronto: Douglas & McIntyre, 2001.

Larry Goodson, *Afghanistan's Endless War: State Failure, Regional Politics, and the Rise of the Taliban*. Seattle: University of Washington Press, 2001.

Michael Griffin, *Reaping the Whirlwind: The Taliban Movement in Afghanistan*. Sterling, VA: Pluto, 2001.

John Hamilton, *Operation Enduring Freedom*. Edina, MN: Abdo, 2002.

Giles Kepel, *Jihad: The Trail of Political Islam*. Trans. Anthony Roberts. Cambridge, MA: Harvard University Press, 2002.

Christina Lamb, *The Sewing Circles of Herat: A Personal Voyage Through Afghanistan*. New York: HarperCollins, 2002.

Tom Lansford, *A Bitter Harvest: U.S. Foreign Policy and Afghanistan*. Aldershot, Hants, England: Ashgate, 2003.

Latifa, with Sheékéba Hachemi, *My Forbidden Face: Growing Up Under the Taliban*. Trans. Linda Coverdale. New York: Hyperion, 2001.

Ralph Magnus, *Afghanistan: Mullah, Marx, and Mujahid.* Boulder, CO: Westview, 2002.

William Maley, *The Afghanistan Wars.* New York: Palgrave, 2002.

———, ed., *Fundamentalism Reborn?: Afghanistan and the Taliban.* New York: New York University Press, 1998.

Eric Margolis, *War at the Top of the World: The Struggle for Afghanistan, Kashmir, and Tibet.* New York: Routledge, 2000.

Peter Marsden, *The Taliban: War and Religion in Afghanistan.* New York: Zed Books, 2002.

Ahmed Rashid, *Taliban: Militant Islam, Oil, and Fundamentalism in Central Asia.* New Haven, CT: Yale University Press, 2000.

———, *Taliban: The Story of the Afghan Warlords.* London: Pan, 2001.

Betsy Reed, ed., *Nothing Sacred: Women Respond to Religious Fundamentalism and Terror.* New York: Thunder's Mouth, Nation Books, 2002.

Rosemarie Skaine, *The Women of Afghanistan Under the Taliban.* Jefferson, NC: McFarland, 2002.

Mary Smith, *Before the Taliban: Living with War, Hoping for Peace.* Aberdour, UK: IYNX, 2001.

Sreedhar, *Taliban and the Afghan Turmoil: The Role of USA, Pakistan, Iran, and China.* New Delhi, India: Himalayan Books, 1997.

Periodicals

Mark Helprin, "What to Do in Afghanistan and Why," *Wall Street Journal*, October 3, 2001.

Charles Krauthammer, "Not Enough Might," *Washington Post*, October 30, 2001.

George Melloan, "Lining Up the Targets on Bush's Hit List," *Wall Street Journal*, November 20, 2001.

Courtland Milloy, "As Taliban Falls, U.S. Confronts New Foe: Itself," *Washington Post*, November 18, 2001.

Michael Renner, "Lessons of Afghanistan: Understanding the Conditions That Give Rise to Extremism," *World Watch*, March 2002.

Time, interview with Osama bin Laden, "Conversation with Terror," January 1999.

Internet Sources

CNN, "Transcript of Bin Laden's October Interview," February 5, 2002. www.cnn.com.

Revolutionary Association of the Women of Afghanistan (RAWA), "Afghanistan: The Taliban's Smiling Face," March 2003. www.rawa.org.

Video

National Geographic, *Afghanistan Revealed*, Warner Home Video, 2001.

Web Sites

Academic Info, www.academicinfo.net. This Web site provides links to many other sites with information about the war in Afghanistan and about Afghanistan's economy and health care and education systems.

Civic Concepts International, www.civicconcepts.org. This site seeks to promote cultural understanding and communication among young people from different countries, in particular with Western countries and war-torn countries such as Afghanistan.

11 September, 2001, www.11-Sept.org. This site offers the latest information about the terrorist attacks and the reasons that they occurred, including information about Afghanistan and the Taliban.

Human Rights Watch, www.hrw.org. This site tracks the health and quality of life of people living in countries such as Afghanistan where human rights abuses are known to occur.

UC Berkeley Library, www.lib.berkeley.edu. This Web site offers detailed information about U.S. policy on Afghanistan.

Washington Post World Afghanistan, www.washingtonpost.com. This site includes up-to-date news articles and opinion pieces written by *Washington Post* journalists about the situation in Afghanistan.

Index